Childhood Dreams

Childhood Dreams

A Book of Crib Quilt Projects

Susan Bennett Gallagher

A Sterling/Main Street Book
Sterling Publishing Co., Inc.   New York

For H.C.M.

Text Design by Ronald R. Misiur

10 9 8 7 6 5 4 3 2 1

A Sterling / Main Street Book

Text, photographs, and quilt designs
© 1989 by Susan Bennett Gallagher
Published by Sterling Publishing Company, Inc.
387 Park Avenue South, New York, N.Y. 10016
Distributed in Canada by Sterling Publishing
℅ Canadian Manda Group, P.O. Box 920, Station U
Toronto, Ontario, Canada M8Z 5P9
Distributed in Great Britain and Europe by Cassell PLC
Artillery House, Artillery Row, London SW1P 1RT, England
Distributed in Australia by Capricorn Ltd.
P.O. Box 665, Lane Cove, NSW 2066
Manufactured in the United States of America

Sterling ISBN 0-8069-7343-9 (Trade)
          0-8069-7342-0 (Paper)

Contents

Introduction

QUILTED MATERIALS are as practical as they are elegant. Two layers of cloth, carefully stitched together and lightly stuffed, make a strong, warm, and decorative fabric. It is not surprising that such materials have a long history and many uses. They show up as robes in ancient Egyptian carvings, as rugs in prehistoric Russian tombs, as coverlets on medieval Sicilian beds, and as underskirts in Elizabethan petticoats.[1]

Patchwork quilts—those bedspreads composed of small scraps of cloth—have a much shorter history. They are an American achievement, closely tied to America's history and reflective of its customs and values. The evolution of these patchwork quilts, and especially of the small ones made just for babies, is an interesting and evocative story.

Colonial Quilts and Their English Origins

American quilts have direct ancestors in seventeenth-century England. There, Elizabethan merchants imported a fine printed cotton cloth called *chintz* from India. Its colors were brilliant and its dyes were colorfast. Chintz was fashionable and expensive.[2] Even the scraps left over after a dress had been cut were hoarded. Enterprising seamstresses soon came up with a use for the leftovers. They cut out the printed figures—the flowers, birds, and animals—and stitched them onto whole pieces of plain-colored local cloth. The largest element would go in the center, with the smaller pieces, usually garlands and birds, framing it in a hierarchical composition. This technique, known as *broderie perse* (Persian embroidery), fulfilled two goals at the same time. The costly decorated chintz was extended to cover a full blanket, and a sort of shortcut instant embroidery was accomplished.[3] These blankets were early versions of appliquéd quilts, appliqué being the technique in which a small piece of material is sewn directly on top of a larger one.

Other seamstresses devised another use for their chintz scraps. They gathered them up, trimmed them into triangles and squares, and sewed them together to make large mosaic-like sheets. The large sheets were backed with full lengths of plain material, stuffed with bits of wool, and the whole ensemble stitched together. These bedcovers were pieced quilts. Piecework is the technique in which many small cloth elements are sewn together to produce a larger piece.

While these chintz spreads were fashionable, they were never essential. The cotton trade with India was always secondary to England's own well-developed wool industry and to Europe's ample linen production. Lacking the push of necessity, England's quiltwork never developed far beyond those Elizabethan efforts.

Early America took its cues from England. Colonial housewives, like their English sisters, saved their scarce imported fabrics. Since England controlled the lucrative textile trades among its colonies, and since the Americans were forbidden to make their own cloth, the fabrics were even scarcer and more costly in America than they had been in England.[4] A broderie perse crib quilt, c. 1825 (figure 1), shows the arrangement established by English traditions—a basket of flowers is ringed by garlands. Another quilt, from the same period, is an example of the piecework style (figure 2). Typically, quilters of these bedcovers used their fancy fabrics on the front and backed them up with a common woolen homespun material.

Only their small size identifies these as children's quilts. Some scholars, including Philippe Ariès and Anita Schorsch, have suggested that the

FIG. 1. Flowers and Birds, c. 1825, probably from Baltimore, 34″ x 36″. Printed chintz and muslin. (*Photo courtesy of the Baltimore Museum of Art; Gift of Linda and Irwin Berman, St. Simon Island, Georgia.*)

FIG. 2. Variable Star, c. 1825, found in New York, 43″ x 32″. Eighteenth-century printed fabric and glazed chintzes. (*Photo courtesy of the Baltimore Museum of Art; Gift of Linda and Irwin Berman, St. Simon Island, Georgia.*)

seventeenth- and eighteenth-century societies of England and America considered children to be just like adults, only smaller.[5] They propose that a combination of factors, including high infant mortality, lack of public education, and the early preparation of children for adult jobs, prevented the sentimental indulgence that has been associated with childhood from the nineteenth century on. Whether or not it is possible to read such cultural attitudes from simple artifacts, it is nonetheless true that these small quilts are nearly identical to the adult versions—no particular themes, techniques, colors, or designs mark them as children's pieces.

Pioneers and Settlers in the Nineteenth Century

American independence was followed by a century of exploration and growth. Pioneers and travelers pushed against the edges of the wilderness to settle in the midwestern and western territories. On their way, these settlers and farmers faced frequent hardship and abundant toil. Women worked alongside men at the plow and in the field. In the evenings, they cooked, cleaned, and raised children. At night, when the day's work was done, the women pieced together fabric from their scrap bags to make quilt squares, and sewed the squares together to make quilt tops. The final step, joining the top to the backing with thousands of tiny stitches, might be done by the woman alone, or it might be done by a party of women in a social event known as a quilting bee.

In this culture, quilting was a necessity, a virtue, and an opportunity. The cold nights and scarcity of material made quilts indispensible. Beyond that, quilts expressed a combination of traits prized by the frontier settlers. Economy, frugality, and efficiency met with patience, charity, and community in the task. And for women quilting was an opportunity to mingle tradition and invention in an artifact of enduring practicality. So often women's work was short-lived. Meals were eaten the same day, and gardens were gone in a season. Women did not usually make buildings or furniture. So the quilt, which might be passed through several generations, or even through a community as a form of payment,[6] acquired a certain permanence and continuity.

Most pioneer quilts were geometrically patterned piecework, made up of square, rectangular, and triangular elements (figures 3 and 4). Sometimes curved elements were used (figure 5), but, as they required more material to make and more skill to sew, they were less common. Piecing was the most economical of all techniques. In its use of repeated identical blocks, it was also the most simple and democratic. By themselves, the square units were small and could be made one at a time, in even the most cramped quarters. An elaborate overall design could be achieved through the manipulations of adjacent blocks.

The patterns were referential. They alluded to pioneer life and artifacts,

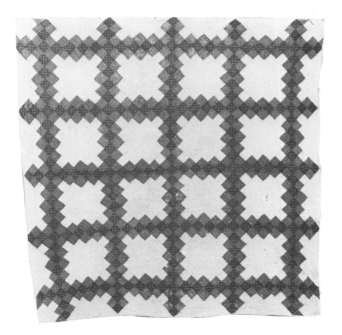

to tools and construction, to food and travel.[7] Log Cabin (figure 6), Carpenter's Square (figure 7), and Corn and Beans (figure 8) were just a few of the designs drawn from everyday life. Occasionally the designs were representational, but the constraints of the technique limited pictorial work to a few patterns. Stars (figure 9) were the most common representational motif, and baskets must have been second, but clever seamstresses also devised a rather graceful flower, the Carolina Lily (figure 10). Frequently, a pattern would have different names in different regions. Thus the arrangement known as Duck's Foot to Long Island's shore communities was called Bear's Paw by Ohio's forest settlers and Hand of Friendship by Philadelphia's Quakers.

The patterns were usually executed in contrasting colors—dark and light patches alternating in stark arrangements. Blue and white pairings are particularly common, white being the natural color of the wool, cotton, or linen fabric, and blue the result of the successful indigo dyes. Other colors were harder to achieve. Green and yellow dyes were unstable and red dyes, expensive. But the simple colors were used to great effect. The bluntness of the combinations recalls the light and shadow of outdoor work and the pleasures and adversity of the pioneer effort.

Some pieced quilts have special optical properties. They are illusionistic. They may imply that the surface of the quilt is three-dimensional, that it has depth and shadow. Or they suggest motion and turbulence. With these quilts, the pattern is ordinary: it is the asymmetric arrangement of color or tone that creates the illusion. Tumbling Blocks (also named Baby Blocks, figure 11) is probably the best known optical design. In it, dark,

FIG. 3. Double Irish Chain, 1840, 48″ x 49″. (*Photo courtesy of the Brooklyn Museum; Gift of the Jason and Peggy Westerfield Collection.*)

FIG. 4. Wild Goose Chase, nineteenth century, 40″ x 39.5″. Printed cottons and brown chintz. (*Photo courtesy of the Smithsonian Institution.*)

Fig. 5. Orange Peel, mid-nineteenth century, 44″ square. (*Photo courtesy of the Brooklyn Museum; Gift of the Jason and Peggy Westerfield Collection.*)

Fig. 6. Log Cabin, c. 1860, 43″ x 30″. (*Photo courtesy of the Smithsonian Institution.*)

Fig. 7. Carpenter's Square, 1844-1854, made by Esther Wileman for Flora, 50.5″ x 47.5″. (*Photo courtesy of the Smithsonian Institution.*)

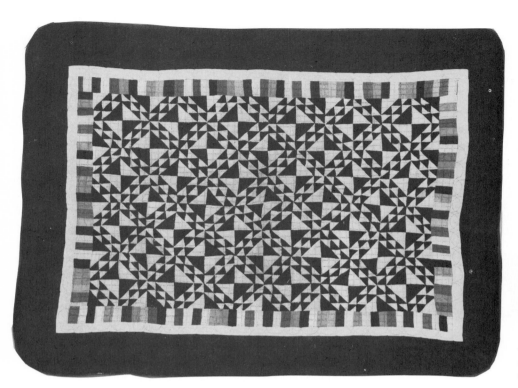

FIG. 8. Corn and Beans (also called Lady in the Lake), c. 1915, 41″ x 30″. Cotton sateen cloth. (*Photo courtesy of the Baltimore Museum of Art; Gift of Linda and Irwin Berman, St. Simon Island, Georgia.*)

FIG. 9. Ohio Star, c. 1913, made by Polly Bontrager, Yoder Corner, Indiana, 48″ x 38″. Pieced and hand quilted cotton. (*Photo courtesy of the Permanent Collection of the Museum of American Folk Art; Gift of David Pottinger.*)

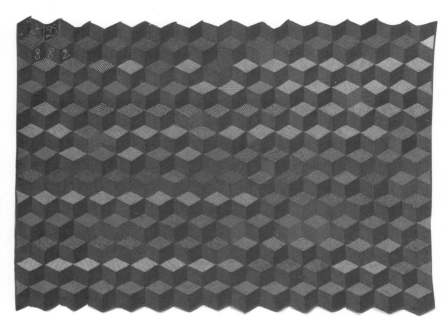

FIG. 10. Carolina Lily, c. 1920, Amish, Holmes County, Ohio, 47″ x 32″. (*Photo courtesy of the Baltimore Museum of Art; Gift of Linda and Irwin Berman, St. Simon Island, Georgia.*)

FIG. 11. Tumbling Blocks, 1882, dated and signed I. A. D., 24″ x 36″. Wool. (*Photo courtesy of the Baltimore Museum of Art; Gift of Linda and Irwin Berman, St. Simon Island, Georgia.*)

medium, and light tones are arranged to suggest a three-dimensional surface. If the diamond-shaped blocks were colored differently, the quilt might resemble stars or flowers instead. Other optical designs, like the one in figure 12, rely on only two colors to create an ambiguous and tense surface.

Along the frontier, infancy was almost too brief to celebrate. Crib quilts were always a bit of a luxury, always rare. Most babies slept in their cradles under folded blankets, or cut-down sections from larger quilts (figure 13). The pieced crib quilts that *were* made, however, are extremely interesting. Most often they are perfectly scaled miniatures. Both the quilt and the constituent blocks were shrunk to infant size. The Tiny Triangles quilt (figure 14), with 1,008 triangles, illustrates this: it shows many scraps were incorporated in a single crib quilt and how tiny the scraps were. No particular patterns or colors were favored for children. Log Cabin, Bethlehem Star, and Bow Tie appear in both large and small versions.

Appliqué quilts were less economical than pieced ones. When money, time, and space allowed, appliqué work might be used for a "best" quilt. In general, appliqué designs are more flexible and more pictorial than others. There are some standard elements, such as double hearts, plumes, wreaths, and leaves, which appear on many quilts. There are also recurring themes which appear with a wide range of individual variation. Flowers, stars, and patriotic motifs are characteristic. Religious subjects occur occasionally. Mostly from the South, and often the work of slave women, these highly individual pieces feature crosses, crowns, and other Biblical references.

Appliqué crib quilts shared some design elements with adult quilts—

Fig. 12. Orange and Black, unknown pattern, 1920-1940, Amish, Mrs. Jacob Miller, Shipshewana, Indiana, 40″ x 30.5″. Pieced and hand quilted cotton. (*Photo courtesy of the Permanent Collection of the Museum of American Folk Art; Gift of David Pottinger.*)

Fig. 13. Cut down quilt, nineteenth century, 40″ x 32″. Cotton. (*Photo courtesy of the Germantown Historical Society, Philadelphia, Pennsylvania.*)

Fig. 14. Tiny Triangles, c. 1850, Lehigh Valley, Pennsylvania, 39″ x 35″. Cotton. (*Photo courtesy of the Baltimore Museum of Art; Gift of Linda and Irwin Berman, St. Simon Island, Georgia.*)

for example, hearts and flowers (figure 15). The technique was accommodating, and many pieces incorporate personal messages and announcements. The Stars and Stripes quilt from Kansas (figure 16) features popular patriotic devices, indicators of both the awakening national identity and the growing influence of national politics on frontier communities. But it also has the word "Baby" written in its largest star. It raises the obvious question, Who was "Baby"? Even more obscure is the message on the Heart and Hat quilt (figure 17). Below the appliqué heart, written in ink, is the following verse:

> *A heart I send, Young Squire Baldwin*
> *Reject it not I do implore thee*
> *A warm reception may it meet*
> *My name a Secret I must keep.*

The appliqué technique lent itself to pictorial work, and, for the first time, special children's themes can be identified in quilts made after the middle of the nineteenth century. Alphabets and schoolhouses, perhaps reflecting the growth of public education, are common. Sometimes the lettered blocks are combined with simple pictures of common objects, like saws, ladders, and scissors. The quilt in figure 18 is almost like a lesson, with its alphabet and images resembling a reading primer. Other quilts used the alphabet alone or were finished with a heart or some other device.

FIG. 15. Floral appliqué, c. 1845, probably from Pennsylvania, 33″ x 34″. Cotton. (*Photo courtesy of the Permanent Collection of the Museum of American Folk Art; Gift of Joel and Kate Kopp.*)

FIG. 16. "Baby," c. 1861, 37″ square. (*Photo courtesy of the Permanent Collection of the permanent collection of the Museum of American Folk Art; Gift of Phyllis Haders.*)

FIG. 17. Heart and Hat, c. 1850, 35″ x 33″. Cotton and wool with black ink inscription. (*Photo courtesy of the Baltimore Museum of Art; Gift of Linda and Irwin Berman, St. Simon Island, Georgia.*)

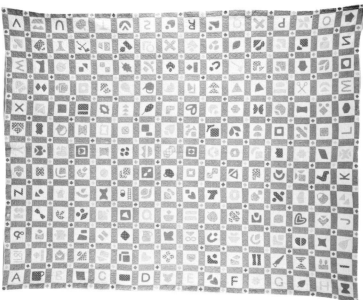

FIG. 18. Alphabet, 1871, 77″ x 62″. (*Private collection; photo courtesy of Thos. K. Woodard American Antiques and Quilts.*)

Amish Quilts

The quilts of Amish women, which were produced concurrently with the examples already mentioned, stand out as a special category. They distinguish themselves with a plainness of pattern that is made electric by a richness of color. In addition, they sometimes feature exceptional stitching.

Deliberately plain, intensely private, and very religious, the Amish settled to farm in Pennsylvania, Ohio, Indiana, and Iowa. They were content to work their quilts with the simplest of elements: large rectangles (figure 19), plain squares, or broad stripes (figure 20). In general they avoided the fancier diamond- and hexagon-shaped elements used by non-Amish quilters; they also avoided the minuscule repetition and ornamentation that characterized certain other pioneer quilts.

The glowing colors are the most striking aspect of the Amish works. Without prints, which the Amish regarded as vain and unnecessary, the solid colors take on a new dimension, depth, and resonance. The Amish

FIG. 19. Inside Border Pattern, 1913, Amish, probably from Ohio, 48″ x 35″. Pieced and hand quilted cotton. (*Photo courtesy of the Permanent Collection of the Museum of American Folk Art; Gift of David Pottinger.*)

were not afraid to use very dark colors—navy blues, browns, and purples are standard — realizing that the darkest colors can make the lighter ones more vibrant. In some cases, the lighter elements even appear to float above the darker field.

Industrialization, Cities, and the Victorian Tradition

While the nineteenth century saw exploration and settlement in the West, it was also a time of industrialization and urbanization. Industrialization gathered people into cities, where they lived and worked indoors.

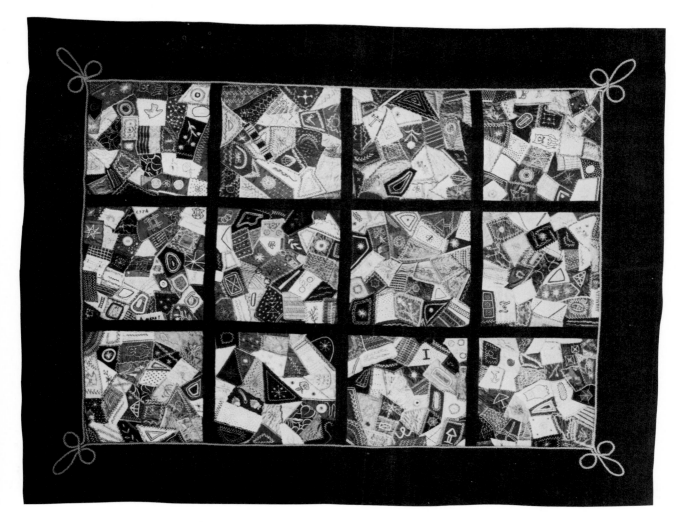

Fig. 21. Crazy Quilt, 1882, 60″ x 76″. Feather stitching and embroidered emblems. (*Photo courtesy of the Smithsonian Institution.*)

The Victorian ideal was an urban life, comfortable, warm. It was epitomized by the parlor, a decorated, ornamented room for small social gatherings and afternoon entertainments.

Machine-made blankets and bedspreads were available, and quilting was no longer a necessity. Instead, it was cultivated as a hobby, something that ladies might do for their amusement and improvement. Quilts became parlor dressing, ornamental pieces of needlework. Fragile fabrics—satins, velvets, and brocades—were favored, and a whole assembly might be embroidered with flowers, spiders, and other emblems (figure 21). The harsh contrasts of dark and light, and the strict geometrical organizations so critical to pioneer efforts, were avoided. The quilts were collections of dark tones and shades: black, wine red, dark blue, and gold swatches shone and glistened beside one another. Oriental fans, associated with the contemporary fascination with Japan and China, were common (figure 22). Crazy quilts, made from wild arrays of overlapping irregular elements (figure 23), were also in vogue.

Fig. 22. Oriental Fans, c. 1880, made by Martha Ada Mumma, Sharpsburg, Maryland, 52.5″ x 51″. Silk and velvet. (*Photo courtesy of the Smithsonian Institution.*)

Fig. 23. Crazy Patchwork with Boxer Dog, 1890-1910, 31″ x 24.5″. Silk, velvet, and lace with silk embroidery. (*Photo courtesy of the Permanent Collection of the Museum of American Folk Art; Gift of Margaret Cavigga.*)

Fig. 24. Alice in Wonderland, 1945, Marion Whiteside Newton, New York, 36″ x 54″. Cotton. (*Photo courtesy of the Metropolitan Museum of Art, Edward C. Moore Fund, 1945.*)

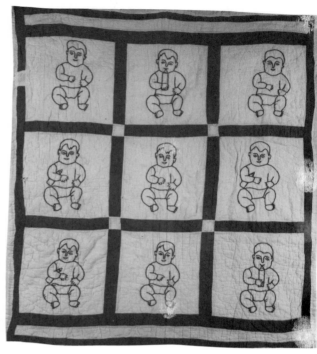

The Victorians regarded childhood as a time of innocence and purity. The nursery was an important room, a sanctum filled with lace and embellished linen. Childhood had its own books, themes, and secrets, which were expressed in nursery rhymes and fairy tales. Figures from these tales show up on crib quilts from this period, and continue to appear in twentieth-century works. Thus Alice, the quintessential Victorian child, appears with Wonderland characters on one quilt (figure 24), while the Gingham Dog and the Calico Cat sit side by side on another (figure 25).

Some designs were influenced by newspapers and advertisements—both achieving wide circulation for the first time. The baby boys from Texas (figure 26) represent a new direction in quilt design: they are line drawings, not appliqué or piecework. Executed in red yarn, the figures resemble those that appear in the comic pages. Advertising images, taken from billboards, labels, and magazines, also appear in works from the early part of the twentieth century. The quilt in figure 27 features Grace Drayton's Campbell Kids in a variety of innocent adventures—the same kids who appeared in advertisements for Campbell's Soup.

The Twentieth-Century Decline

In the early twentieth century there were more factories, more goods, more money, and fewer reasons to make quilts than ever before. Quilts, like other homemade products, were sometimes associated with poverty and

Fig. 27. Campbell's Soup Kids, c. 1920, probably from Massachusetts, 42″ x 32″. Cotton cloth with cotton embroidery, hand quilted. (*Photo courtesy of Laura Fisher.*)

Fig. 28. Red Crazy, 1987, made by Jan Myers, 41.5″ x 54.5″. Cotton. (*Photo courtesy of Jan Myers,* © 1987.)

backwardness, a source of shame or embarrassment.[8] Grandmothers and great-grandmothers continued the traditions that they had learned as girls, but quilting was in decline.

There was a sputter of enthusiasm in the 1930s, perhaps related to the poverty of the Depression and to the theme of the heroism of labor which was part of the recovery. The National Park Service even developed a quilting program to assist rural women. Quilt patterns were recorded in several books at the time and quilt kits were introduced.[9] But the enthusiasm faded quickly and vanished by the time of World War II.

Contemporary Quilting

Only recently have old quilts been recognized as the great and original works that they are. A seminal show at the Whitney Museum of Art in 1971 pushed hundreds of the finest quilts into the public eye.[10] Other museums arranged exhibitions. Collectors took note and scholars did research. Books and articles appeared. The Whitney show also contributed to a surge in quiltmaking, modern and experimental. The constraints that earlier quilters had endured were no longer applicable. Modern quilters enjoy an abundance of fabric and other materials; they have ample working space; they have helpful machines. They also benefit from scientific processes and techniques which could not have been imagined by our quilting ancestors. They can use photographic transfer technology to print photographs on cloth; they can use airbrushes, paints, and reliable dyes for color; they can even use graphic computers to fine-tune their patterns and designs.

Many new quiltmakers are studio artists who abandoned painting or sculpture in favor of quilting. They treat quilts like canvases done in fabric, and they try to locate their works in the artist's domain.

Modern quilting themes vary widely. Some quilts explore the old issues of contrast, light, and shade, but they replace the repetitive blocks that characterized earlier quilts with changing blocks. Their makers are colorists, working with finely graded and subtle color distinctions. Other quilters use collision and impact in their work: different traditional patterns collide and recombine to create new designs. Still others, like Jan Myers, create modern crazy quilts, with very tightly controlled and organized "crazy" elements (figure 28).

Other quilters make figurative quilts. The figures range from the abstract and allegorical to the intensely personal. The artist Faith Ringgold's "100 Pounds Weight Loss" quilt documents her own struggles with diets: she uses it as an element in a performance she gives on the same topic. Her other works deal with her family and the Harlem neighborhoods in which she grew up. The Men: Mask Face Quilt #2 (figure 29) combines painting, silkscreen, and quilting in one such piece.

A Personal Approach to Quiltmaking

The challenge of history is to learn from it, to experiment with it, to build on it. The history of quilting is so rich in technique and so varied in content that there is limitless room for invention. A quilt can be a literal true-to-tradition piece; it can use a modified or reinvented design; or it can be completely experimental, incorporating new materials and technologies.

I like to work with simple elements and materials, so most of my quilts are fairly straightforward. They use standard materials, printed and solid cotton cloth, joined by hand and by machine. (I use a sewing machine whenever I can, and I feel quite certain that my quilting ancestors would have done the same if machines had been available to them.) Most of my quilts are rectangular, but some are square. Many are inspired by traditional designs, but they are not slaves to historical precedent.

I am particularly interested in three traditions of quilts—the geometric, the pictorial, and the crazy—and it is to these types that I have directed most of my efforts. I should say right away that not all my efforts have been successful: my closets are filled with single squares, small panels of designs, or combinations that just did not work.

The geometric tradition is the most celebrated of the quilting categories. In general, geometric designs are the easiest to make and therefore are a good place for a beginning quilter to start. The clean lines and strict patterns allow the designer to explore some of the basic ideas of pattern and color.

In my geometric quilts I have investigated some of the following questions:

Should the quilt be dark or light? The Pinwheels quilt (Project 15) is a dark one, but most of my quilts fall into a middle ground, neither light nor dark. Does the quilt have high-contrast colors, or does it use a range of evenly graded tones? My Leaves quilt (Project 7) uses tones, while the Nine-Patch design (Project 3) works with contrasting colors. I find contrast easier to establish than a tonal pattern.

Why are the traditional two-color blue and white quilts so successful? In a two-color arrangement, do the two colors appear in equal or unequal amounts? What effects do printed fabrics have on the overall pattern? Does the quilt design make a continuous net over the quilt surface, as in the Waves quilt (Project 14), or are there clearly defined, independent units as in the Apple Pie quilt (Project 12)? What about geometric quilts with three or four colors, like Fence Rail (Project 11)? Can the colors be used to create the illusion of depth, or of light and shadow? How do the colors work together? What about curves? How do curves meet each other, how do they join? In the Watermelons quilt (Project 10), each block has three concentric curves, but the curves do not join across the blocks. In the Waves quilt, the undulating pattern depends on the continuity of adjacent arcs across the surface.

What about those odd geometric quilts that actually look like objects? As has been previously noted, picture quilts are rare in the geometric tradition, but both the Waves and the Watermelons quilts are pictorial.

And finally, are there simpler ways to make complicated patterns? Which designs can be assembled from a series of fabric strips? In this collection of quilts, the Nine-Patch lends itself to strip assembly, but the other projects do not.

The pictorial tradition relies chiefly on appliqué work. Appliqué requires more hand sewing and is usually slower and more difficult than geometric quilting. Like the geometric quilts, my appliqué projects study a range of questions.

Is the quilt one picture, like an oil painting, with a top and bottom, sides, and a single subject? Or is it a pictorial pattern, an arrangement

Fig. 30. Moon and Stars, 1985, made by Susan Bennett Gallagher, 36″ square. Cotton. (*Photo courtesy of Susan Bennett Gallagher,* © 1985.)

of repeating elements on a neutral surface? Contemporary quilts, especially those designed to hang on a wall rather than lie on a bed, often adopt the former attitude. I prefer the latter, and all my appliqué quilts have arrangements of repeating blocks. How do the blocks relate to each other, and to the whole quilt? Are the blocks square? Rectangular? Is the quilt square or rectangular? Most of my quilts are rectangular—Grapevines, Ducks and Umbrellas, Hearts and Hands (Project 5, 6, and 8)—but occasionally the theme dictates a square shape. The Moon quilt (figure 30) is square because the phases of the moon follow a regular, even cycle.

What about colors for the pictorial elements? Do the pictures rely on color and line for definition, or are they just silhouettes? Silhouettes, like the rabbits in Rabbits and Carrots (Project 2) and the hands in Hearts and Hands, are the easiest to appliqué. Figures with internal seam lines (color lines) are harder to make. For example, the ducks in Ducks and Umbrellas have white bodies with yellow beaks and feet. Should the figures be colored "naturally," or can other colors be used? I have found that if the figure is going to be a silhouette, it can be done in almost any strong color. If the figure is to be subdivided into separate color areas, realistic colors work best.

Crazy quilts are my current interest. I find them the hardest to understand, the most challenging of all the quilts to design.

What makes a quilt crazy? Is it a profusion of colors? The Crazy Blocks quilt (Project 4) cycles twelve different colors through a single irregular block, but the Crazy Quilt (Project 9) limits itself to a minimal palette of four colors. Can a two-color quilt be a crazy quilt? The quilt in figure 31 is just that: a two-color crazy quilt, done in traditional blue and white fabrics. Does a crazy quilt need a wide range of element sizes? Is asymmetry important? Do the elements overlap each other, as they do in classic crazy designs, or can they be pieced together like geometric patterns? Does the randomness of the pattern recognize any borders or edges, or does it just slam into the quilt boundaries? What about printed materials in crazy quilts? Do they strengthen or weaken the effect?

And what about the ornamental stitching and embroidery that show up on so many Victorian quilts? How is the embroidery designed, and what do the figures mean?

———————————

What challenges, what opportunities!

Each question raises another, and each completed quilt generates ideas for ten new designs.

Quilting is wonderful. Enjoy it.

Susan Bennett Gallagher
December 1, 1989

Fig. 31. Crazy, 1985, made by Susan Bennett Gallagher, 36″ x 48″. Cotton. (*Photo courtesy of Susan Bennett Gallagher,* © 1988.)

Notes

1. See *Crib Quilts and Other Small Wonders,* Thomas K. Woodard and Blanche Greenstein (New York: E. P. Dutton, 1981).
2. See *English Chintz,* Frank Lewis (Essex, England: F. Lewis Publishers, 1973).
3. See *The Pieced Quilt,* Jonathan Holstein (New York: Galahad Books, 1973).
4. Ibid.
5. See *Centuries of Childhood, a Social History of the Family,* Phillipe Ariès, translated by Robert Baldick (New York: Vintage Books, 1962) and *Images of Childhood,* Anita Schorsch (Pittstown, N.J.: The Main Street Press, 1985).
6. See *The Quilters: Women and Domestic Art,* Patricia Cooper and Norma Bradley Buferd (New York: Doubleday and Company, 1977).
7. See "The Quiltmaker's Landscape," Dolores Hayden and Peter Marris (*Landscape* Magazine, New York: December, 1981).
8. See *The Perfect Patchwork Primer,* Beth Gutcheon (Baltimore: Penguin Books, Inc., 1973).
9. Ibid.
10. See *Abstract Designs in American Quilts,* Jonathan Holstein (New York: The Whitney Museum of American Art, 1973).

Metric Equivalency Chart

INCHES TO MILLIMETRES AND CENTIMETRES
MM — Millimetres   CM — Centimetres

INCHES	MM	CM	INCHES	CM	INCHES	CM
⅛	3	0.3	9	22.9	30	76.2
¼	6	0.6	10	25.4	31	78.7
⅜	10	1.0	11	27.8	32	81.3
½	13	1.3	12	30.5	33	83.8
⅝	16	1.6	13	33.0	34	86.4
¾	19	1.9	14	35.6	35	88.9
⅞	22	2.2	15	38.1	36	91.4
1	25	2.5	16	40.6	37	94.0
1¼	32	3.2	17	43.2	38	96.5
1½	38	3.8	18	45.7	39	99.1
1¾	44	4.4	19	48.3	40	101.6
2	51	5.1	20	50.8	41	104.1
2½	64	6.4	21	53.3	42	106.7
3	76	7.6	22	55.9	43	109.2
3½	89	8.9	23	58.4	44	111.8
4	102	10.2	24	61.0	45	114.3
4½	114	11.4	25	63.5	46	116.8
5	127	12.7	26	66.0	47	119.4
6	152	15.2	27	68.6	48	121.9
7	178	17.8	28	71.1	49	124.5
8	203	20.3	29	73.7	50	127.0

YARDS TO METRES

YARDS	METRES	YARDS	METRES	YARDS	METRES
⅛	0.11	3½	3.20	6⅞	6.29
¼	0.23	3⅝	3.31	7	6.40
⅜	0.34	3¾	3.43	7⅛	6.52
½	0.46	3⅞	3.54	7¼	6.63
⅝	0.57	4	3.66	7⅜	6.74
¾	0.69	4⅛	3.77	7½	6.86
⅞	0.80	4¼	3.89	7⅝	6.97
1	0.91	4⅜	4.00	7¾	7.09
1⅛	1.03	4½	4.11	7⅞	7.20
1¼	1.14	4⅝	4.23	8	7.32
1⅜	1.26	4¾	4.34	8⅛	7.43
1½	1.37	4⅞	4.46	8¼	7.54
1⅝	1.49	5	4.57	8⅜	7.66
1¾	1.60	5⅛	4.69	8½	7.77
1⅞	1.71	5¼	4.80	8⅝	7.89
2	1.83	5⅜	4.91	8¾	8.00
2⅛	1.94	5½	5.03	8⅞	8.12
2¼	2.06	5⅝	5.14	9	8.23
2⅜	2.17	5¾	5.26	9⅛	8.34
2½	2.29	5⅞	5.37	9¼	8.46
2⅝	2.40	6	5.49	9⅜	8.57
2¾	2.51	6⅛	5.60	9½	8.69
2⅞	2.63	6¼	5.72	9⅝	8.80
3	2.74	6⅜	5.83	9¾	8.92
3⅛	2.86	6½	5.94	9⅞	9.03
3¼	2.97	6⅝	6.06	10	9.14
3⅜	3.09	6¾	6.17		

Designs for
Fifteen
Crib Quilts

General Notes

1. Use 100 percent cotton fabrics. Synthetic materials and blends can be unpredictable and may deteriorate over time.

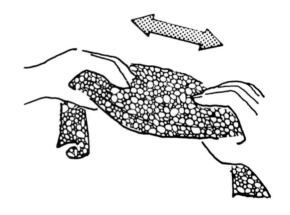

2. Test material by pulling on it (gently) in several directions. It should hold its shape well. If it stretches, the quilt pieces will stretch before they are sewn, and it will be harder to sew them together.

3. Pick prints carefully. Small calico prints, like #1, are the easiest to work with. One-way prints, like #2, can be difficult. If they don't all point in the same direction (and in a quilt, they probably won't), they can be visually disturbing. Try to use materials with different tones or values. Print #3 is considerably darker than print #4. Combining these two fabrics should make the quilt surface more interesting and lively.

4. Wash and iron all fabrics before cutting or sewing.

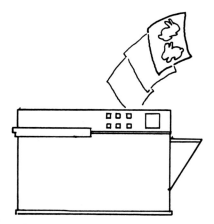

5. Copy patterns from the book. They can be traced onto cardboard or duplicated on a copier machine. Some of the older copier machines distort images slightly; be careful that the machine reproduces images accurately.

6. Cut and measure all pieces carefully. The more accurately the material is cut, the easier it will be to assemble the quilt.

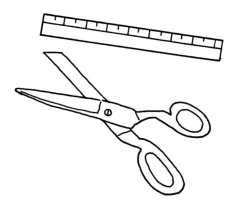

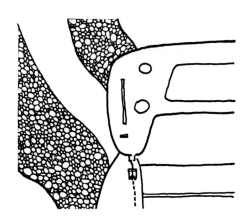

7. Appliqué work is generally done by hand. Piecing can be done by hand or with a machine. Seam allowances are ¼″ unless noted otherwise. Seam allowances can be trimmed or clipped if the pieces are small or very curved.

8. The quilt can be filled with either cotton batting or polyester batting. Cotton batting is thinner, flatter, and a bit easier to work with. Polyester makes a puffier, thicker quilt. The choice between polyester and cotton is mostly a question of preference, although if the surface becomes too puffy, it may detract from the overall quilt design.

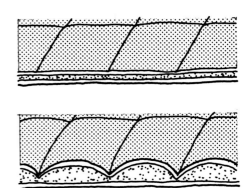

10. Do not use buttons on a quilt which is to be used by infants or young children. Buttons can be hazardous. Eyes for animals can be made easily from small circles of cloth, appliquéd to the duck or rabbit.

9. After the quilt is finished, check it carefully for pins. Remove all pins.

11. Do not worry if the quilt is not absolutely perfect. Some seams may not meet exactly; some edges may be slightly askew. The quilt does not have to be perfect to be special.

Give the quilt to a special baby!

1. Alphabet

The alphabet as a theme for children's quilts first appeared around the end of the nineteenth century. Its appearance coincided with the growth of public education, and its development paralleled the establishment of children's readers and primers.

Because the theme was never standardized, each alphabet quilt has a unique organization. Some of the best versions combine plain schoolbook lettering with a wide range of images and patterns.

The alphabet quilt of this project uses bold, rather old-fashioned blue letters as a border. The images are carefully chosen so that each letter corresponds to at least one picture. At the same time, there is an ambiguity about the images, and double readings are possible. In some cases, there is an extra level of organization in which certain squares relate to their neighbors. A hammer is located next to a group of nails, a hand reaches for an ice-cream cone, and an owl sits on a branch under a crescent moon.

The colors are not bright. The picture blocks use maroons, greens, reds, blues, and browns on light calico squares, randomly distributed. The backgrounds for the letters are also pale calicoes, but they are more organized: light red blocks alternate with very light green ones around the border. The quietness of the colors allows the images—the profiles of the pictures and shapes of the letters—to dominate the arrangement. The colors also recall those used in early textbooks—McGuffey readers with their brown and sepia tones.

The quilt is tacked rather than quilted. Blue yarn at the intersections of the squares superimposes a pattern over the jumble of images and gives depth to the surface of the "page." The tacking also adds a kind of no-nonsense utilitarian quality to the quilt.

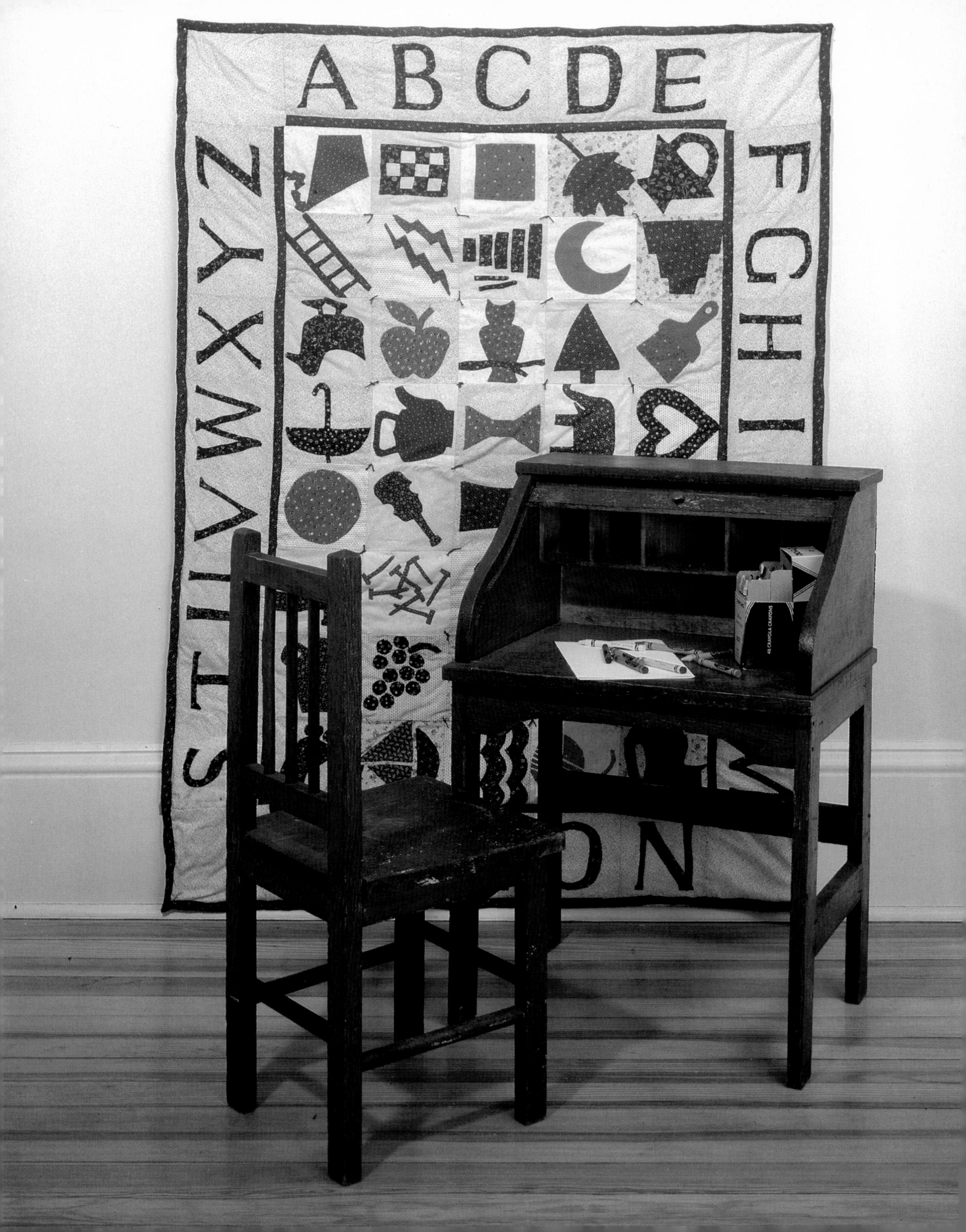
A B C D E
F G H I
S T U V W X Y Z
O N

Instructions

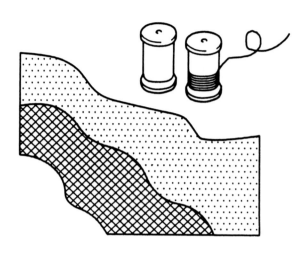

1. Materials:

   2 yards green print (backing and underline strips)
   ¾ yard blue print (letters)
   ½ yard light red print (letter background squares)
   ½ yard very light green print (letter background squares)
   1 yard of mixed light prints (background squares)
   ¾ yard of mixed dark prints (pictures)
   Cotton batting
   White thread
   Heavy blue thread or yarn for tacking

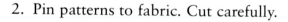

2. Pin patterns to fabric. Cut carefully.

   Cut a long edge strip, 2″ wide and 16′ long, from the green material.

   Cut two underline strips, 1″ wide, 25½″ long, from the green material.

   Cut two underline strips, 1″ wide, 40½″ long, from the green material.

3. Pin the picture elements to the background squares. Hand stitch along seam lines. Clip as required at curves and corners. Note that some of the pictures are made of two or more parts.

   The picture elements have no particular color assignments, and neither do their background squares.

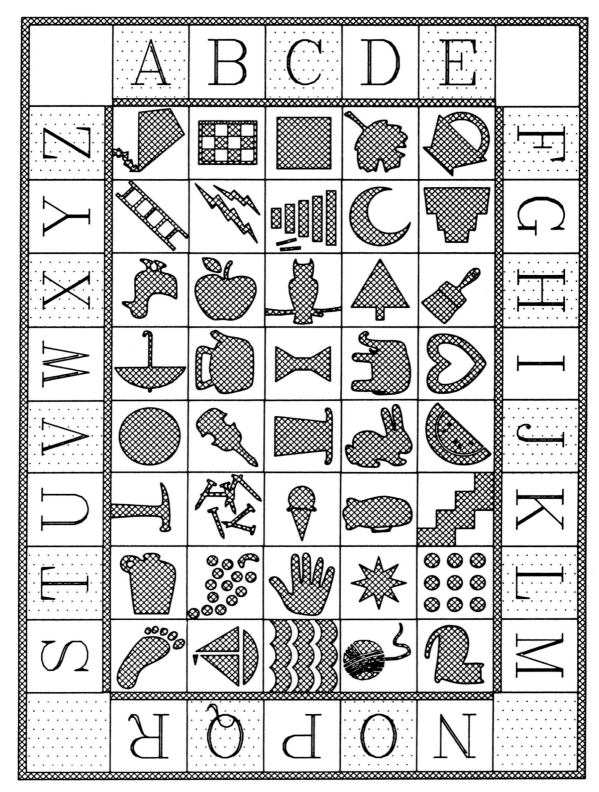

Finished quilt, 36" by 52"

4. Pin the letters to their background squares. The letters are dark blue, but the background squares alternate between a light red print and a light green print. "A" and "F" start on the light red. "N" and "S" start on the light green.

5. With a machine, sew together the rows of picture blocks. Assemble the rows, matching seams carefully.

6. Sew the letter blocks together.

   A-E is the first row.

   F-M is the second row.

   N-R is the third row.

   S-Z is the fourth row.

   Sew the four green underline strips to the rows of letter blocks.

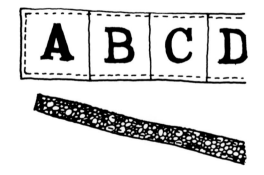

7. Sew the two light green corner squares to the ends of the A-E strip.

   Sew the two light red corner squares to the ends of the N-R strip.

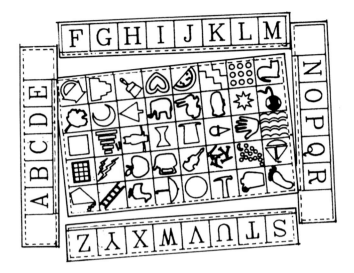

8. Complete the quilt top by sewing the letter borders to the picture block assembly.

9. Lay the quilt backing, face down, on a large table or work area. Lay the batting on top of it. Lay the quilt top, face up, on the batting. Pin through all three layers. Machine stitch along the edge of the quilt top. Trim close to the seam.

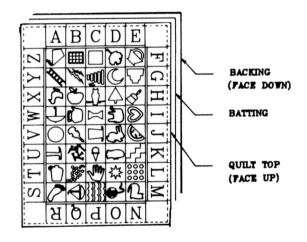

BACKING
(FACE DOWN)

BATTING

QUILT TOP
(FACE UP)

10. Press the seam allowances of the edge strip under. Hand stitch the strip around the quilt assembly.

11. Quilt stitch along both sides of the underline strips. Tack the rest of the quilt at the corners of the picture blocks.

Pattern Pieces

Shown one-half actual size

Cut 2, light red, and 2, light green

Cut 13, light red, and 2, light green

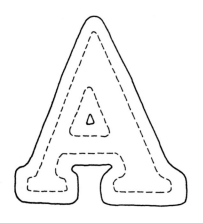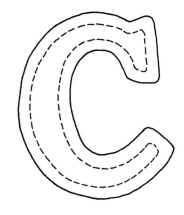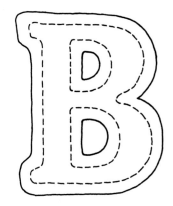

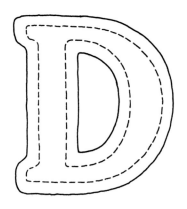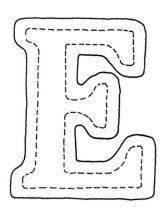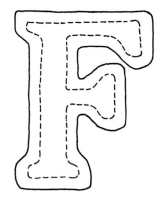

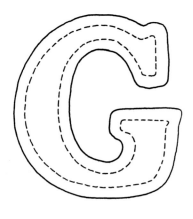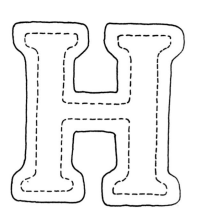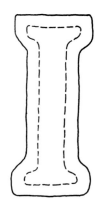

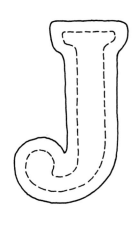 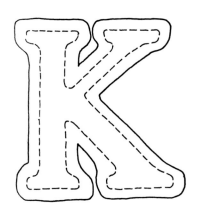 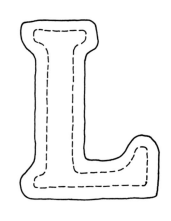

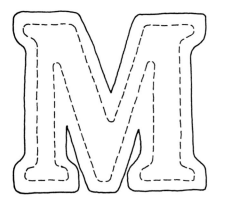 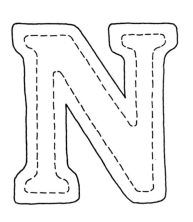 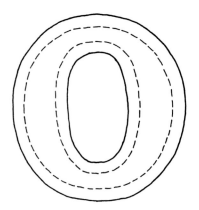

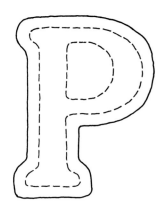 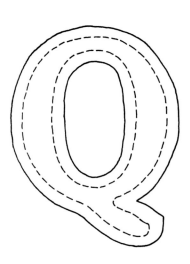 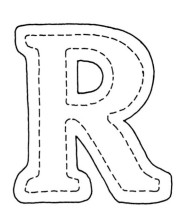

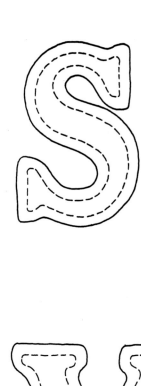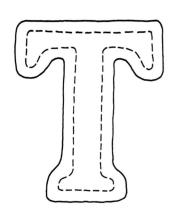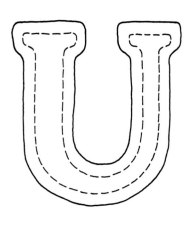

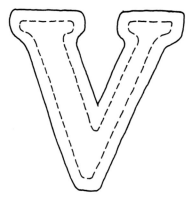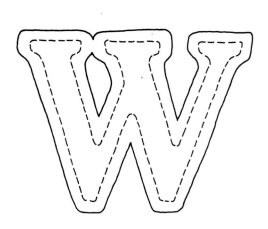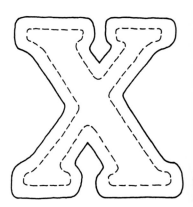

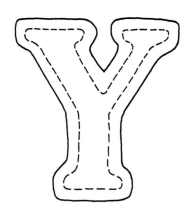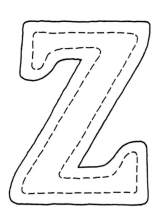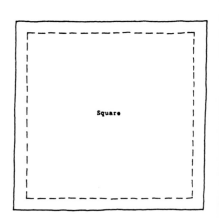

Square

Lightning

Lightning

Basket

Top hat

Zeppelin

Moon

Heart

Teakettle

Owl

Bow tie

Kite

Ladder

Rabbit

Boat pennant

Boat sail

Boat sail

Ice-cream

Boat

Ice-cream cone

Waves, cut 3

Yarn

Star

Zigzag

Grape stem

Duck

Grapes, cut 13

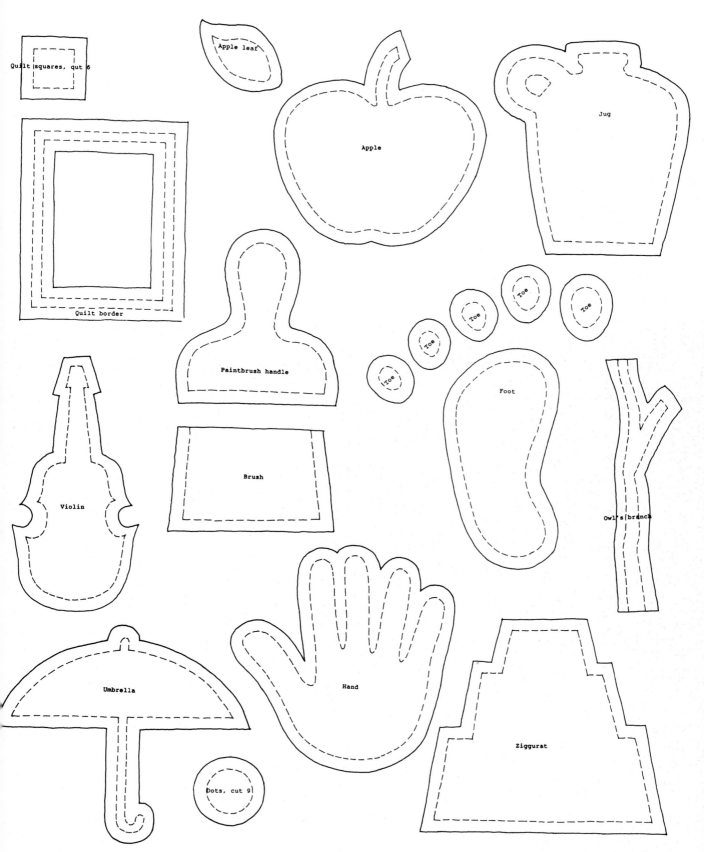

Quilt squares, cut 6

Apple leaf

Apple

Jug

Quilt border

Paintbrush handle

Toe

Toe

Toe

Toe

Toe

Foot

Violin

Brush

Owl's branch

Hand

Umbrella

Dots, cut 9

Ziggurat

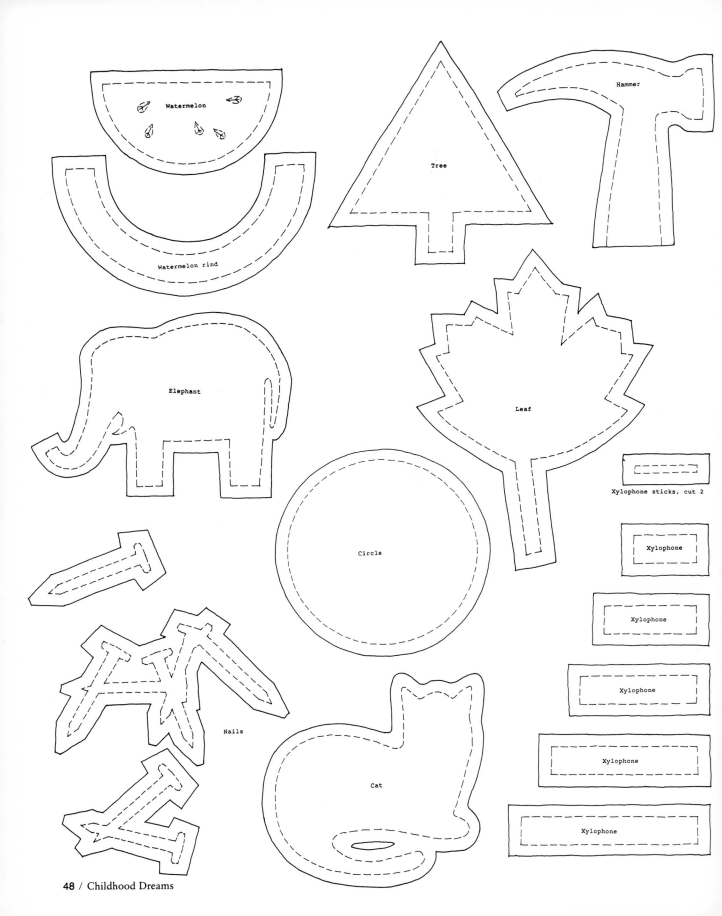

Watermelon

Watermelon rind

Tree

Hammer

Elephant

Leaf

Xylophone sticks, cut 2

Circle

Xylophone

Xylophone

Xylophone

Nails

Xylophone

Cat

Xylophone

2. Rabbits and Carrots

Rabbits have a time-honored spot in the nursery, and children's stories are filled with them. There is Peter Rabbit, the Velveteen Rabbit, Br'er Rabbit, Bugs Bunny, and the bunnies in *Goodnight Moon*. All these rabbits are somewhat mischievous, very clever, and usually set off against parents or other adults, with whom they are reconciled by story's end.

Rabbits have very distinctive profiles. The ears and the tails contribute to the strong graphic image. In contrast, carrots have simple shapes and vibrant coloring.

This quilt locates dark blue appliquéd rabbits in a carrot patch. The rabbits face each other across green lattice strips. The organization of the rabbits acknowledges the rectangular shape of the quilt, but it does not distinguish between "top" and "bottom" or "left" and "right."

The rabbits are partly camouflaged in their field; their blue matches the print of the background squares. The carrots, bunched three to a square, are border elements. They unfold around the rabbits, thereby locating them in the patch. This organization is a classic device. It resembles that seen in some Egyptian paintings, where palm trees unfold around lotus-filled pools. The same device is found on early maps, where city walls unwrap to reveal the city within.

Finished quilt, 36" by 48"

Instructions

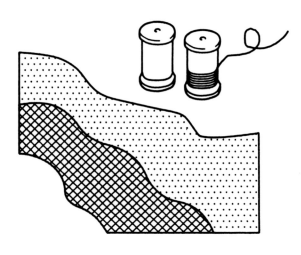

1. Materials:

   2½ yards blue print (rabbits and lattice strips)

   ½ yard green print (carrot tops and lattice strips)

   ½ yard orange print (carrots and lattice squares)

   1½ yards white and blue print (background squares)

   Cotton batting

   White, orange, green, and blue thread

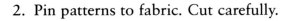

2. Pin patterns to fabric. Cut carefully.

   Cut a long edge strip, 2" wide and 14' long, from the blue material.

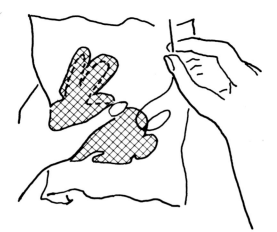

3. Pin rabbit to background square. Beginning next to the ears, hand stitch along seam line. Clip as required at curves and corners. Appliqué stitch the carrots and carrot tops to background squares. The carrot tops should be sewn first. The carrots will overlap the tops.

4. With a machine, sew together the rows of squares by alternating the appliqué squares with the lattice strips.

   Sew together the rows of strips, alternating the lattice strips with the lattice squares.

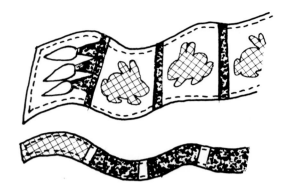

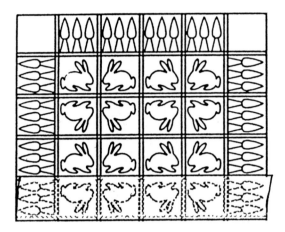

5. Assemble the quilt top by sewing together the rows of squares and strips, matching all seams carefully.

6. Lay the quilt backing face down on a large table or work area. Lay the batting on top of the backing. Lay the quilt top, face up, on the batting. Pin through all three layers. Machine stitch along the edge of the quilt top. Trim close to the seam.

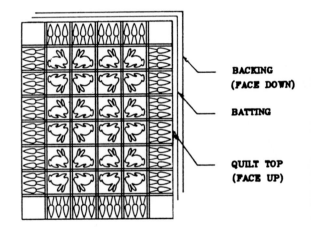

BACKING
(FACE DOWN)

BATTING

QUILT TOP
(FACE UP)

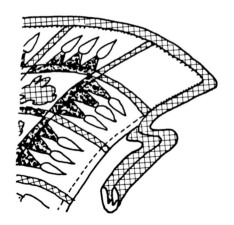

7. Press the seam allowances of the edge strip under. Hand stitch the strip around the quilt assembly.

8. For quilting, outline stitch around the rabbits and carrots, either by hand or with a machine.

Pattern Pieces

Shown one-half actual size

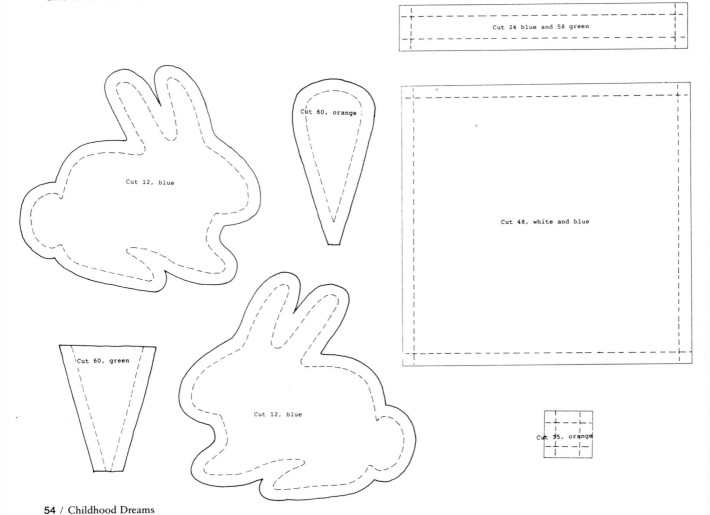

Cut 24 blue and 58 green

Cut 60, orange

Cut 12, blue

Cut 48, white and blue

Cut 60, green

Cut 12, blue

Cut 35, orange

3. Nine-Patch

Old handmade quilts were additive. Each small piece was sewn to its neighbors to make a block, then the block units were joined to make the quilt top. The block was the critical unit, the molecule of the quilt, from which the properties and design of the overall spread could be envisioned.

Many patterns that were handmade, piece by piece, in earlier times can be sewn by machine today. The efficient technique for machine construction is typically quite different from the hand-sewing system. It can be a real challenge to adapt a moderately complicated pattern such as this nine-patch variation to a machine system.

The machine technique is not an additive process; it is a reductive one in which the overall quilt pattern is not revealed until near the end of the construction. The operational unit is the strip. Initially, the fabric is cut into strips of varying widths and lengths. The strips are sewn together and then cut into new strips. Subsequent operations sew the strips and then cut new ones until the entire quilt top is assembled. The whole procedure is a sort of abstract sequence, rather like a computer program.

The strip technique can be used for all sorts of regular patterns, including ones with triangular, rectangular, and square elements.

Instructions

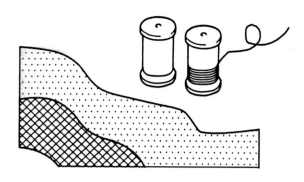

1. Materials:

   1½ yards cream cloth
   3 yards green print
   Cotton batting
   Cream and green thread
   Green string or yarn for tacking

2. Set aside 1½ yards of green cloth for quilt backing.

   Cut the cream cloth into strips:
   7 strips, 1¼″ wide, 30″ long
   8 strips, 2½″ wide, 15″ long
   7 strips 2¾″ wide, 30″ long
   8 strips 2¼″ wide, 30″ long

   Cut the remaining green cloth into strips:
   7 strips, 1¼″ wide, 15″ long
   8 strips, 2½″ wide, 30″ long
   8 strips, 2¼″ wide, 30″ long

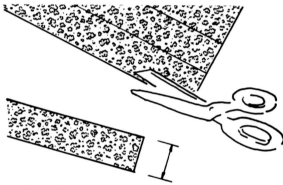

   Border strips:
   2 strips 2¼″ wide, 30¼″ long
   2 strips 2¼″ wide, 46¼″ long

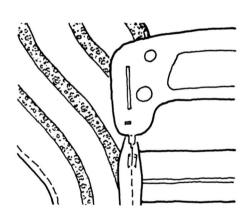

3. Sew the 2½″ wide, 15″ long cream strips to the 1¼″ wide, 15″ long green strips, alternating green and cream.

4. Trim the edges of the cloth just sewn if they are uneven. Measure and cut across the seams as shown. Cut 10 strips, 1¼″ wide.

   These are the "A" strips.

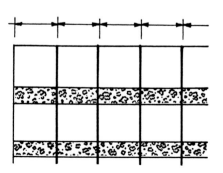

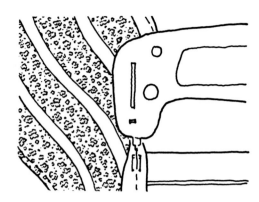

6. Trim the edges of the cloth just sewn if they are uneven. Measure and cut across the seams as shown. Cut 11 strips, 2½" wide.

These are the "B" strips.

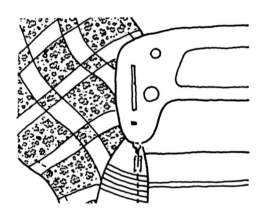

8. The cloth just sewn measures approximately 21" by 30". Trim the edges if they are uneven.

Cut and discard 1¼" strips from both long sides.

Cut the remaining cloth into 7 strips, 2¾" wide. Each strip should be centered on a thin cream line.

These are the "C" strips.

5. Sew the 2½" wide, 30" long green strips to the 1¼" wide, 30" long cream strips, alternating green and cream.

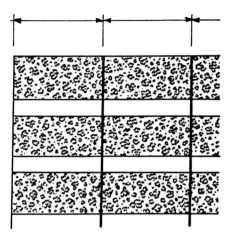

7. Sew the A and B strips together, carefully matching seams.

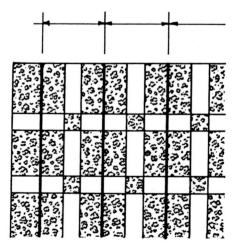

Finished quilt, 33" by 45"

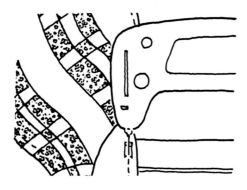

9. Sew the C strips to the 2¼″ wide, 30″ long cream strips.

10. The new cloth will be approximately 30″ by 30″. Trim the edges if they are uneven.

    Cut and discard 1¼″ from each long side.

    Cut the remaining cloth into 10 strips, each 2¾″ wide. Each strip should be centered on a nine-patch element as shown.

    These are the "D" strips.

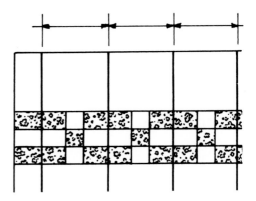

11. There are 8 green and 7 cream strips remaining. Sew them together, alternating colors.

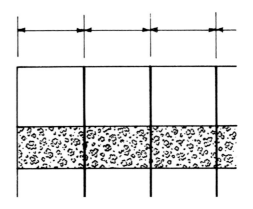

12. Measure and cut across the cloth just sewn.

    Cut 11 strips, 2¼″ wide.

    These are the "E" strips.

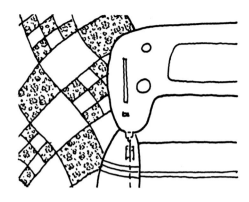

14. To complete the quilt top, sew the green border strip around it.

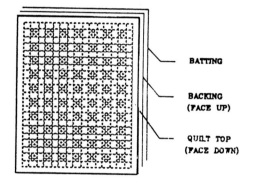

BATTING

BACKING
(FACE UP)

QUILT TOP
(FACE DOWN)

16. Sew around the edges, leaving an 8″ gap at the end. Trim the seams.

Use the 8″ gap to turn the quilt right side out.

Hand sew the 8″ gap closed.

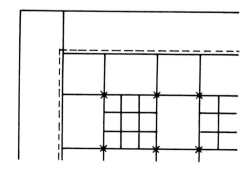

13. Sew the D strips and the E strips together, matching seams as shown.

This is the quilt top, nearly finished.

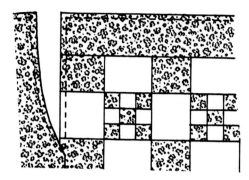

15. On a large table or work surface, lay the quilt batting down. Lay the backing material, face up, on top of the batting. Lay the quilt top, face down, on the backing. Pin around the edges.

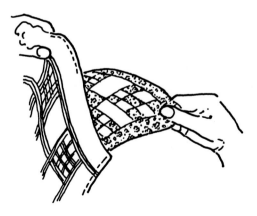

17. Sew through all layers of the quilt close to the edge of the border strip. Using the heavy green thread, tack the layers together at the corners of the nine-patches.

Finished quilt, 40" by 50"

4. Crazy Blocks

Crazy quilts are hard to make. To begin with, they are usually carefully organized and their random appearance is an illusion. The successful ones are like collages, with careful balances of light and shade, decoration and background, size and scale, pattern and texture. It is an interesting coincidence that some of the most sophisticated crazy quilts come from the late nineteenth and early twentieth centuries, when artists were experimenting with planes, surfaces, distortions, and perception. It is as if the quilting women were exploring the same themes with needle and thread that the artists were addressing in their paintings and compositions.

Some quilts are hybrids, combinations of crazy elements and plain ones. Some of the most interesting ones impose the rigor of a geometrical grid over a group of crazy blocks. The practical reason for this type of arrangement is that the crazy blocks are easier to assemble than an entire expanse of fabric. The design consequence is that there is a tension between the grid and the apparently random elements.

Crazy Blocks is a gridded crazy quilt, or a "contained" crazy. The rotated squares alternate with plain wine-red elements, and the whole field is set off with dark blue borders.

For simplicity this quilt uses a single crazy block with nine colors. The blocks appear to be different because the colors are not repeated in the same position from block to block. As is often the case, the craziness is not confusion but complexity. Once the system is understood, the design is clear.

In this quilt the plain dark solids become background elements, while the brightly colored fragments dominate. Ornamental quilt stitching in colored threads around the fragments completes the design.

Instructions

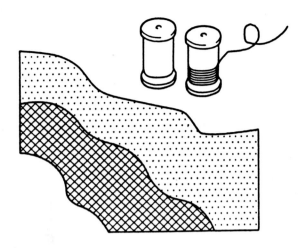

1. Materials:

   2½ yards solid navy blue cloth (backing, borders, and crazy elements)

   1 yard solid maroon cloth (plain squares and crazy elements)

   ¼ yard each of ten solid colors: pale yellow, gold, orange, red, light green, light blue, blue-gray, purple, green, and forest green

   Cotton batting

   Colored thread

2. Set aside 1½ yards of navy blue cloth for backing.

   Cut maroon squares and triangles using pattern pieces. Cut navy blue border pieces:
   2 pieces 5½" wide, 40" long
   2 pieces 5½" wide, 30½" long

   Cut long edge strip from navy blue, 2" wide and 14' long.

   Stack six colors of cloth. Pin pattern pieces 1 to 9 to the stack.

   Cut carefully.

   Stack the remaining six colors of cloth, pin pattern pieces 1 to 9 and cut carefully.

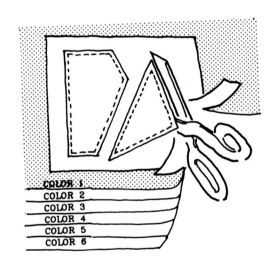

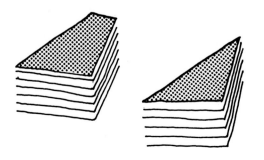

3. Lay the first batch of pattern pieces over the second group. There will be nine stacks, each with twelve colors of materials.

SUSAN GALLAGHER

Crash, 1987
Pieced Fabric

HENRI MATISSE

Le Bateau, 1947
Cut Paper

4. Organize the colors into a "crazy" arrangement by taking the top color of the first stack and moving it to the bottom of the stack. Then take the top two colors of the second stack and move them to the bottom of that stack. Take the top three colors from the third stack, etc., and repeat for each stack until all nine stacks are done.

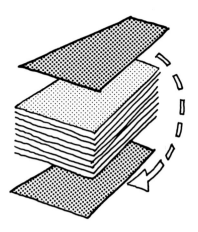

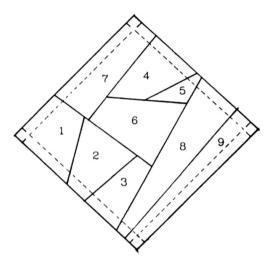

5. Now sew the crazy blocks, using the top colors of the stacks for each of the nine pattern pieces. Each finished block will have a different arrangement and combination of colors.

6. Sew the crazy blocks into strips. Each strip will start with a maroon triangle, and then a crazy block. The shortest strips will end immediately with another maroon triangle. The longer strips will have an alternating sequence of maroon squares and crazy blocks before ending with a maroon triangle.

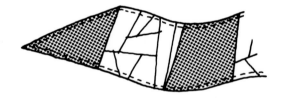

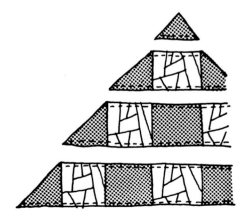

7. Assemble the quilt top by sewing together the rows of squares and crazy blocks, matching all seams carefully.

8. To finish the quilt top, join the 30½″ navy blue pieces with the maroon corner blocks to form the top and bottom border strips. Join these newly created strips and the 40″ side strips to the quilt top.

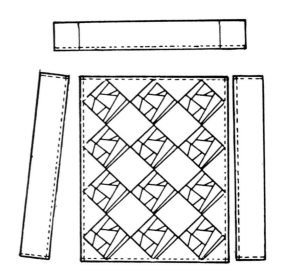

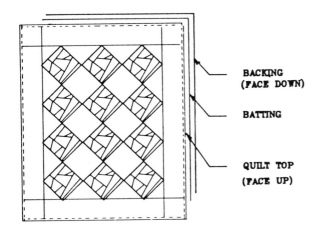

BACKING
(FACE DOWN)

BATTING

QUILT TOP
(FACE UP)

9. Lay the quilt backing, face down, on a large table or work area. Lay the batting on top of the backing. Lay the quilt top, face up, on the batting. Pin through all three layers. Machine stitch along the edge of the quilt top. Trim close to the seam.

10. Press the seam allowances of the edge strip under. Hand stitch the strip around the quilt assembly.

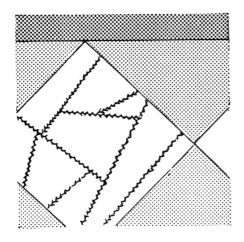

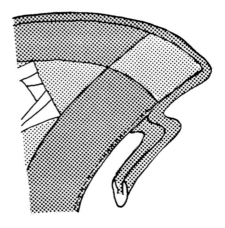

11. For quilting, use a feather stitch or other decorative stitch along the individual elements in each crazy block. Use brightly colored thread.

Crazy Blocks / 67

Pattern Pieces

Shown one-half actual size

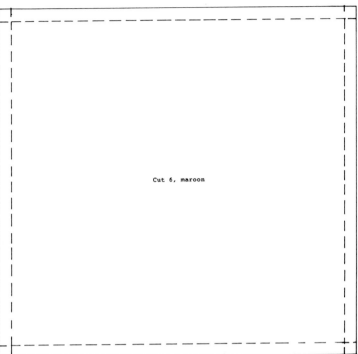

Cut 6, maroon

Cut 4, maroon

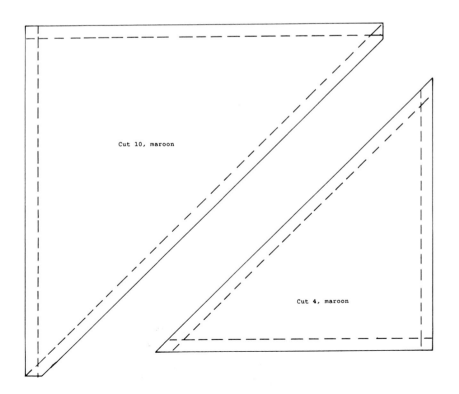

Cut 10, maroon

Cut 4, maroon

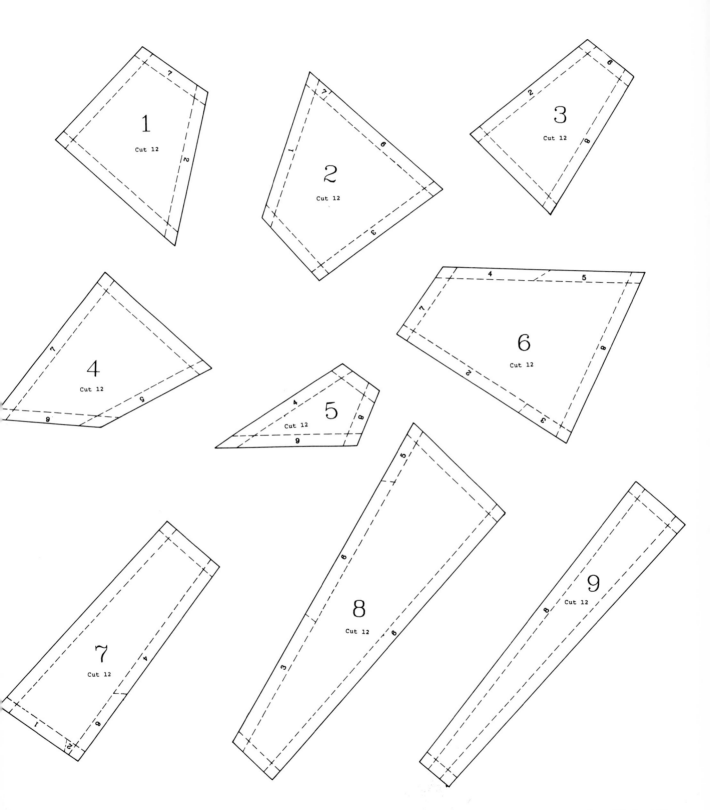

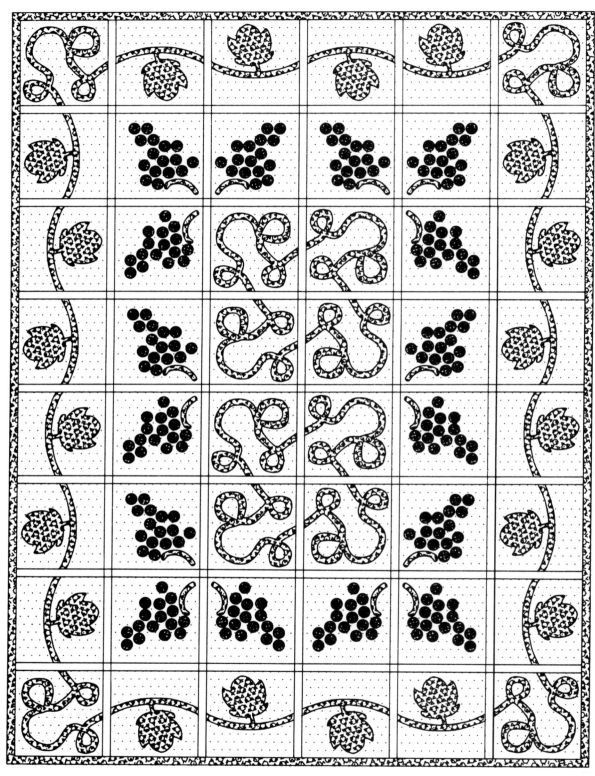

Finished quilt, 36" by 48"

5. Grapevines

Curving vines, ornamented with fruits or flowers, are a traditional quilt motif. They are often used to create a border pattern, like a great wreath framing some scene or display. On these quilts the vines are beautiful. They curve gracefully and the leaves respond to the curves. The flowers or fruits hang like jewels on the ring of vines and leaves.

This quilt honors the vine. The motif is not a secondary element in a larger design. The entire composition uses only three types of blocks. The leaf block is used along the edges, the grape block is found just inside the leaves, and the vine block is used at the center and corners.

Each grape block has a single cluster of grapes, diagonally oriented across the square. The grapes themselves are lightly stuffed and randomly arranged within the cluster. They are done in an assortment of dark blue calico prints. The prints, with their tiny colored shapes, add sparkle and richness to the grapes.

The leaf blocks feature slightly curved vines, with broad leaves fitting into the gentle arcs.

The vine blocks are used to complete the corners, to allow the greenery to make a ring. Corner blocks are often a very difficult proposition, because the block must "face" two different directions. Here, the vine elements are designed to fill the corners in a graceful and satisfying way.

The background for all the blocks is a pale green print, which contrasts with the superimposed white grid. The lattice, made of a heavy white cotton piqué, makes a trellis for all the grapevines.

Instructions

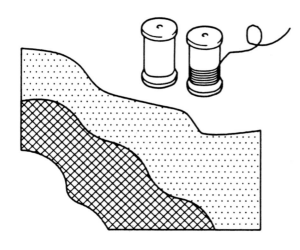

1. Materials:

   2½ yards green print (leaves, vines, and backing)
   ¼ yard mixed blue prints (grapes)
   ½ yard white cotton piqué (lattice strips)
   1½ yards light green print (background squares)
   Cotton batting
   White, green, and blue thread

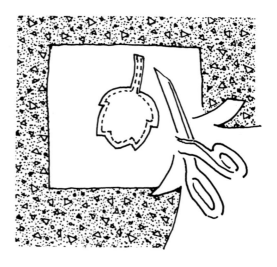

2. Set aside 1½ yards of green print for backing.

   Pin patterns to fabric. Cut carefully.

   Cut a long edge strip, 2″ wide and 14′ long, from the green material.

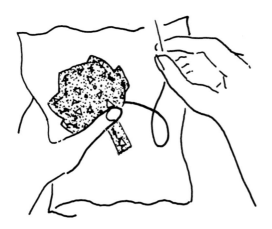

3. Pin leaf to background square. Beginning at end of stem, hand stitch along seam line. Clip as required at curves and corners.

   Pin arced vine element to background square, making sure that the beginning and the end of the vine piece meet the edges of the background squares at the centers. The vine will overlap the leaf stem. Hand stitch along seam lines.

4. Pin curved vine element to background square. The vine should begin and end at the centers of the square edges. Hand stitch along seam lines.

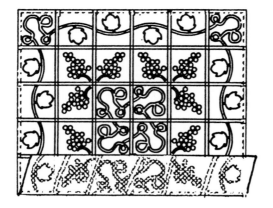

5. Arrange grapes in a cluster formation on background squares. The cluster should have a diagonal orientation, from one corner to its opposite. Using a pencil or dull instrument, insert a bit of stuffing into each partly sewn grape before completing the seam. Sew the grape stem at the corner of the background square, at the top of the bunch.

6. With a machine, sew together the rows of squares by alternating the appliqué squares with the lattice strips.

Sew together the rows of strips, alternating the lattice strips with the lattice squares.

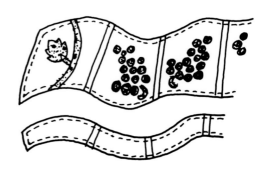

7. Assemble the quilt top by sewing together the rows of squares and strips, matching all seams carefully.

8. Lay the quilt backing face down on a large table or work area. Lay the batting on top of the backing. Lay the quilt top, face up, on the batting. Pin through all three layers. Machine stitch along the edge of the quilt top. Trim close to the seam.

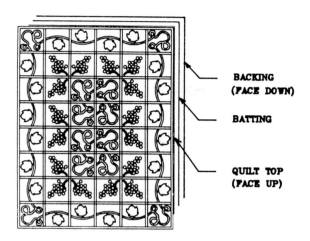

BACKING
(FACE DOWN)

BATTING

QUILT TOP
(FACE UP)

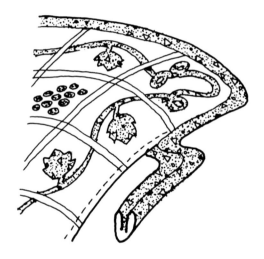

9. Press the seam allowances of the edge strip under. Hand stitch the strip around the quilt assembly.

10. For quilting, outline stitch around the lattice strips, either by hand or with a machine.

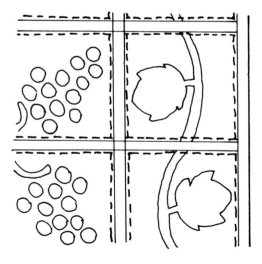

Pattern Pieces

Shown actual size

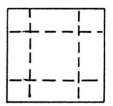

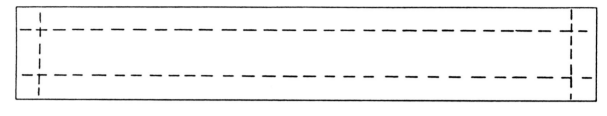

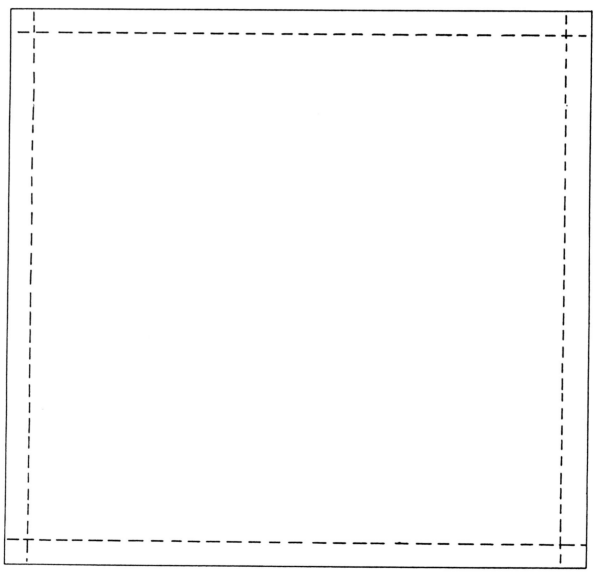

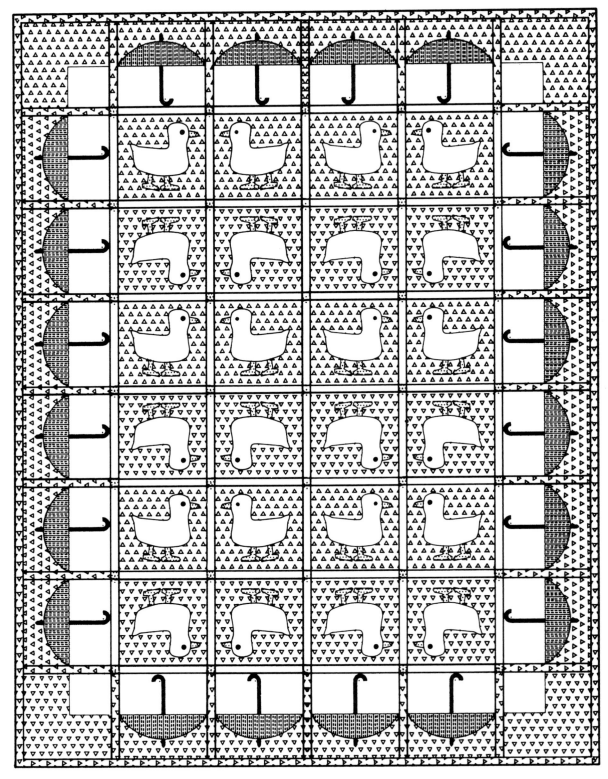

Finished quilt, 36" by 48"

6. Ducks and Umbrellas

Ducks and geese are common characters in children's books. Usually they are depicted as silly, foolish creatures, sometimes because they are playing in the rain, other times because they are chatting with foxes. These characterizations are moralizing ones; their aim is to discourage children from splashing in puddles or from talking to strangers.

On this quilt, ducks are paired with umbrellas and the two figures generate the design. There are two different types of pictorial blocks. One type shows pale ducks in a rainy blue field. The ducks are done in reverse appliqué. Direct appliqué techniques would not work in this case because the pale cloth of the bodies (a "feathery" yellow print on white fabric) is too light to be used on top of the blue background. The bills and feet are made from a bright yellow print. The bills are done in reverse appliqué in order to maintain a continuity of line with the bodies. The feet, which are usually described as gangly and clumsy, are done in direct appliqué. The switch in technique from body to feet emphasizes the awkwardness of the feet.

The umbrella blocks show umbrellas in their classic form. Wide open, broad and black, with dark rain above and light yellow below, they make a protective edge around the quilt. The umbrellas are not completely black. They are a calico print, splashed with small dots that correspond to those in the blue print. This correspondence gives them a kind of rainy sparkle. It is also important to note that the umbrellas do not quite meet—and in the gaps between them, rain pours down.

Instructions

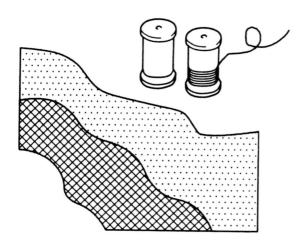

1. Materials:

   3 yards medium blue print (backing
   and duck squares)
   ¼ yard black print (umbrellas)
   1 yard white and yellow print (duck
   squares and lattice strips)
   ¼ yard yellow print (duck bills and feet)
   ¼ yard solid black (umbrella handles
   and lattice squares)
   Cotton batting
   White and blue thread

2. Pin patterns to fabric. Cut carefully.

   Cut a long edge strip, 2″ wide and 14′
   long, from the medium blue material.

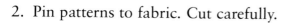

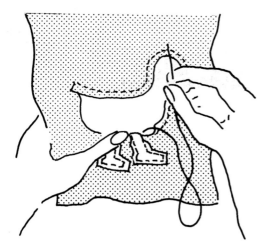

3. Pin duck square over duck background,
   pinning beak cloth in proper location.
   Hand stitch along the seam line. At the
   duck belly, fold the seam allowances for
   the duck feet under and tuck the tops of
   the feet over the belly edge. Sew across
   the tops of the feet. Clip curves and corners as necessary.

   Finish square by sewing across duck bill
   and around duck feet.

4. Sew the blue and white elements of the umbrella squares together. Sew umbrella handles to the squares, then sew umbrellas over handles.

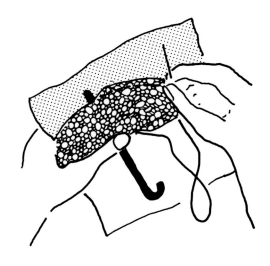

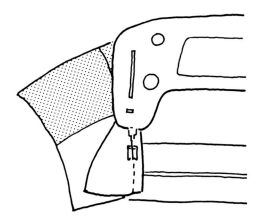

5. The corner squares are made of three small blue squares and a single white square.

6. With a machine, sew together the rows of squares by alternating the appliqué squares with the lattice strips.

Sew together the rows of strips, alternating the lattice strips with the lattice squares.

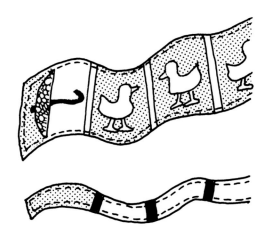

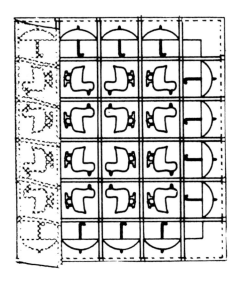

7. Assemble the quilt top by sewing together the rows of squares and strips, matching all seams carefully.

8. Lay the quilt backing face down on a large table or work area. Lay the batting on top of the backing. Lay the quilt top, face up, on the batting. Pin through all three layers. Machine stitch along the edge of the quilt top. Trim close to the seam.

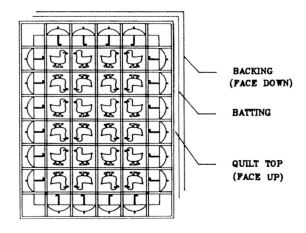

BACKING
(FACE DOWN)

BATTING

QUILT TOP
(FACE UP)

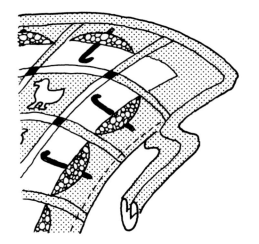

9. Press the seam allowances of the edge strip under. Hand stitch the strip around the quilt assembly.

10. For quilting, outline stitch inside along the tops of the umbrellas and on the inside of the ducks as shown.

Pattern Pieces

Shown one-half actual size

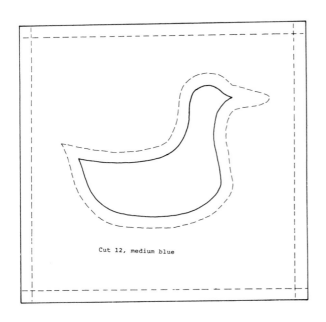

Cut 12, medium blue

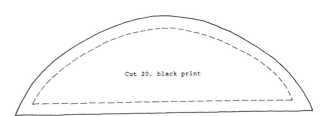

Cut 20, black print

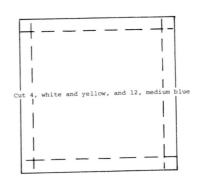

Cut 4, white and yellow, and 12, medium blue

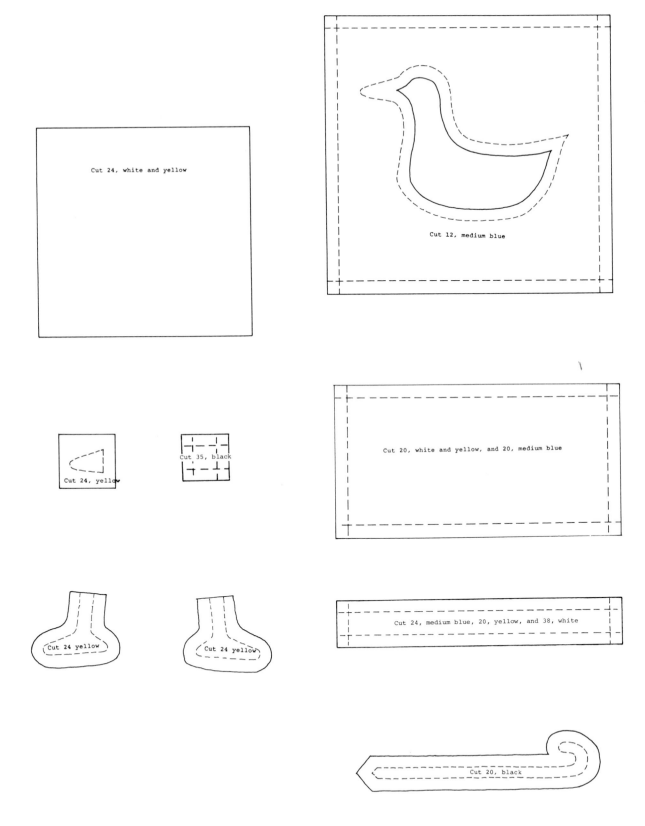

Cut 24, white and yellow

Cut 12, medium blue

Cut 24, yellow

Cut 35, black

Cut 20, white and yellow, and 20, medium blue

Cut 24 yellow

Cut 24 yellow

Cut 24, medium blue, 20, yellow, and 38, white

Cut 20, black

Finished quilt, 36" by 48"

7. Leaves

The Leaves quilt has a two-color nine-patch square as its basic unit, but each square has a different pair of colors. Six colors weave through the quilt in the long direction, while eight different colors cross its width. In each direction the tones start with the greens and pale yellows that represent summer colors. These are followed by the oranges and golds that are part of autumn's palette. The final shades in each direction are the scarlets and dark browns that show up at the end of the season.

The use of tiny elements—there are 432 "leaves"—helps to make a "forest." The arrangement of colors, while it has a dominant direction from green to brown, has a secondary organization in which the early shades mingle with the later ones. This interweaving and grading of tones contributes to a sort of fluttering effect, as if the forest were stirred by wind.

The Leaves quilt was inspired by Amish traditions. Admirers of Amish quilts are always struck by their simplicity of form and richness of color. The stripped-down design, the bareness of the pattern, are essential to this quality. Without fussy forms and complicated prints, the colors attain a vibrancy and intensity that are lacking in certain more complex quilts.

Another interesting fact about Amish work is that it so often contains very dark tones. Dark browns, purples, navy blues, and even black appear in Amish quilts for both adults and children. This use is in distinct contrast to the prevailing opinions of the times, which favored lighter, more "cheerful" shades in works intended for children.

Instructions

1. Materials:

   ¼ yard each of the following solid colors: pale yellow, spring green, emerald green, tan, orange, orange-red, scarlet, brown, forest green, yellow, gold, maroon, light brown, and dark purple

   1½ yards of backing material

   Cotton batting

   Quilting thread in the above colors

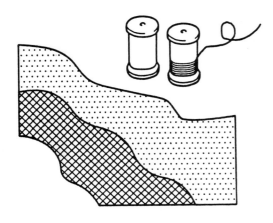

2. Cut 2½″ squares from all the fabrics. Either use the pattern piece or cut 2½″ wide measured strips, and cut again to make the squares.

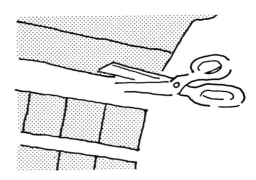

3. The best way to make this quilt is to sew the small squares together to make a series of nine-square blocks. Each block is different from all the others; no two have the same pair of colors.

   The chart shows how the nine small squares are sewn together, and it also identifies the number and color of small squares that make up each block.

A	#1	A
#1	A	#1
A	#1	A

5- A 4-#1	4- A 5-#2	5- A 4-#3	4- A 5-#4	5- A 4-#5	4- A 5-#6
4- B 5-#1	5- B 4-#2	4- B 5-#3	5- B 4-#4	4- B 5-#5	5- B 4-#6
5- C 4-#1	4- C 5-#2	5- C 4-#3	4- C 5-#4	5- C 4-#5	4- C 5-#6
4- D 5-#1	5- D 4-#2	4- D 5-#3	5- D 4-#4	4- D 5-#5	5- D 4-#6
5- E 4-#1	4- E 5-#2	5- E 4-#3	4- E 5-#4	5- E 4-#5	4- E 5-#6
4- F 5-#1	5- F 4-#2	4- F 5-#3	5- F 4-#4	4- F 5-#5	5- F 4-#6
5- G 4-#1	4- G 5-#2	5- G 4-#3	4- G 5-#4	5- G 4-#5	4- G 5-#6
4- H 5-#1	5- H 4-#2	4- H 5-#3	5- H 4-#4	4- H 5-#5	5- H 4-#6

Rows of colors:
   A is pale yellow
   B is spring green
   C is emerald green
   D is tan
   E is orange
   F is orange-red
   G is scarlet
   H is brown

Columns of colors:
   1 is forest green
   2 is yellow
   3 is gold
   4 is maroon
   5 is light brown
   6 is dark purple

4. On a large table or work surface, lay out the 5 squares and 4 squares that will make up each block. This is an important step, as it is very easy to get confused and sew the wrong squares together.

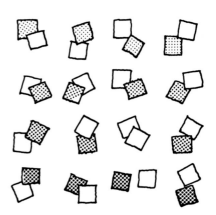

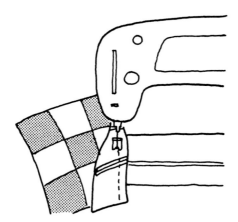

5. Sew the nine-square blocks together using the stacks of small squares from the table. Return each finished block to its place on the table.

6. Sew the blocks together into rows, matching seams carefully.

Assemble the rows to make the quilt top.

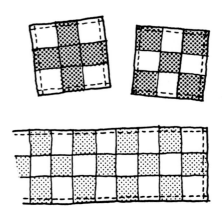

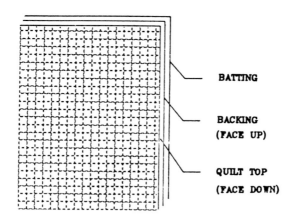

BATTING

BACKING
(FACE UP)

QUILT TOP
(FACE DOWN)

7. Lay the quilt batting on the table or work surface. Lay the backing material, face up, on the batting. Lay the quilt top, face down, on the backing. Pin through all three layers. Sew around the edge, leaving 8″ unsewn at the end. Trim close to seam.

8. Turn the quilt right side out by pulling it through the 8″ gap.

Sew the gap closed by hand.

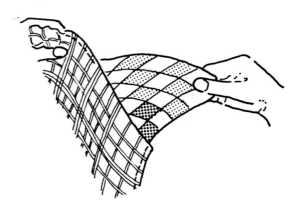

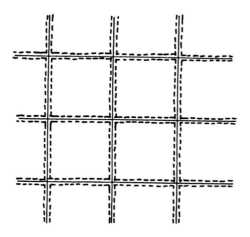

9. For quilting the three layers together, sew around each small square close to its edges. Use thread that matches the square color.

Pattern Piece

Shown actual size

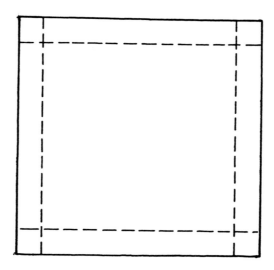

Cut 27 of colors A, B, C, D, E, F, G, H
36 of colors 1, 2, 3, 4, 5, 6

8. Hearts and Hands

Hands and hearts are archetypal human symbols. They make an early appearance in cave paintings from prehistoric times. They continue to appear in painting and sculpture from a range of ages and cultures. Hands express both individuality and community along with care, protection, and creation. Hearts are potent images too. Even before their biological functions were understood, they were singled out as special organs and associated with love, generosity, and friendship.

A crib quilt seems a particularly appropriate place to join the two images, since infants need the protection and care that the two emblems signify.

This quilt uses a palette of reds and blues. The dark blue hands are appliquéd onto light red squares, while the hearts are done in reverse appliqué—bright red on light blue. A medium blue tone, used in the lattice strips, mediates between the two intense colors.

The use of reverse appliqué for the heart squares creates an interesting layering effect at the border, an effect in which the border can be understood in two different ways. The corner squares—light blue, but without the applied red—suggest that the border is a continuous frame around the field, but the red appliqué pieces deny it. They suggest that the field is the result of an intersection, a place where two zones cross.

Finished quilt, 36" by 48"

Instructions

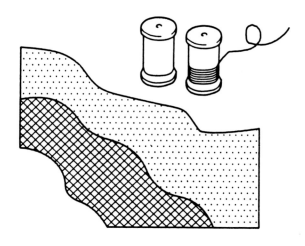

1. Materials:

   2 yards medium blue print (backing and lattice strips)

   ¾ yard red print (hearts and lattice squares)

   ¾ yard light red print (hand background)

   ¾ yard light blue print (heart background)

   ¾ yard dark blue print (hands)

   Cotton batting

   White thread

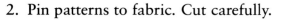

2. Pin patterns to fabric. Cut carefully.

   Cut a long edge strip, 2″ wide and 14′ long, from the medium blue material.

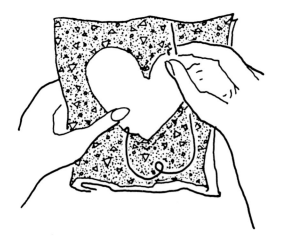

3. Pin heart square over heart background. Hand stitch along the seam line. Clip as required at curves and corners.

   Appliqué hands to hand background squares, beginning next to the thumbs. Clip as required between fingers and along curves.

4. With a machine, sew together the rows of squares by alternating the appliqué squares with the lattice strips.

Sew together the rows of strips, alternating the lattice strips with the lattice squares.

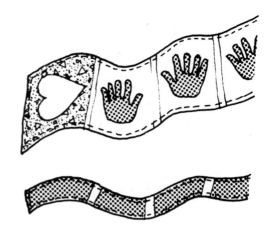

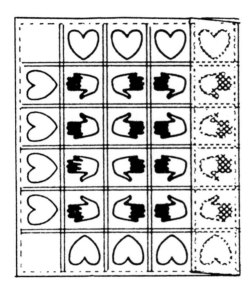

5. Assemble the quilt top by sewing together the rows of squares and strips, matching all seams carefully.

6. Lay the quilt backing face down on a large table or work area. Lay the batting on top of the backing. Lay the quilt top, face up, on the batting. Pin through all three layers. Machine stitch along the edge of the quilt top. Trim close to the seam.

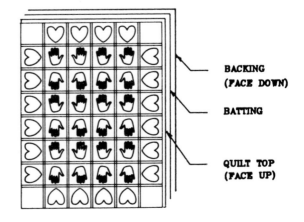

BACKING
(FACE DOWN)

BATTING

QUILT TOP
(FACE UP)

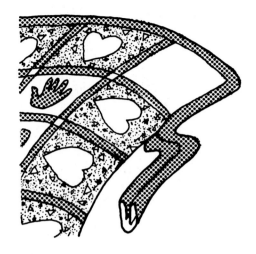

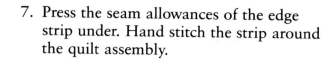

7. Press the seam allowances of the edge strip under. Hand stitch the strip around the quilt assembly.

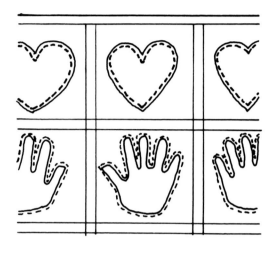

8. For quilting, outline stitch inside the hearts and outside the hands, either by hand or by machine.

Pattern Pieces

Shown one-half actual size

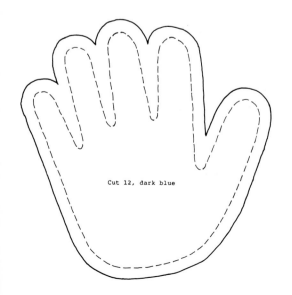

Cut 12, dark blue

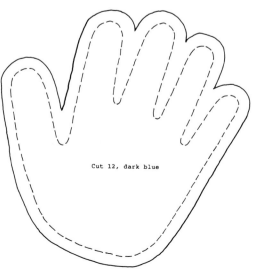

Cut 12, dark blue

Cut 20, red

Cut 24 light blue and 24 light red

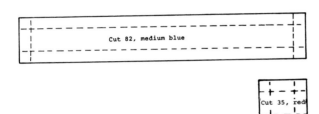

Cut 82, medium blue

Cut 35, red

9. Crazy Quilt

This quilt was inspired by the behavior of light, and by the phenomena of reflection, refraction, and transparency. Light is critical to visual perception; it makes color, shape, and shadow.

The pattern is generated by a net of intersecting straight lines. They are randomly arranged, and the resulting shapes are irregular triangles, quadrilaterals, and other polygons. At the edges the intersecting lines of the net are transformed into a series of parallel lines, as if organized by a laser or prism. At the same time, the irregular shapes become a sequence of regular rectangles and squares.

The surface is colored with four closely related colors: a navy blue, a turquoise, a lavender, and a blue-green. In order to make distinct elements on a flat planar surface, four colors are exactly the right number. Three colors would be inadequate, and a fifth shade would be superfluous. In mathematics this situation is known as the "four-color map theorem." The rigor of the quilt derives from the severity of its geometry and from its strict limitation of colors. The fabrics are solid colors since prints would dilute the design by distracting from the elements and lines.

Like the colors, the quilting stitching reinforces the geometry of the design. Each polygonal shape is quilted along its perimeter (just inside the seam line) in a matching thread.

Instructions

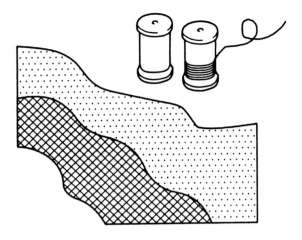

1. Materials:
   ¾ yard each of solid turquoise, green, and lavender
   2½ yards of solid navy blue
   Cotton batting
   Turquoise, green, lavender, and navy blue thread

2. The easiest way to assemble this quilt is to divide it into eight separate zones. Zones 1 through 4 make up the field of the quilt; zones 5 through 8 make up the border.

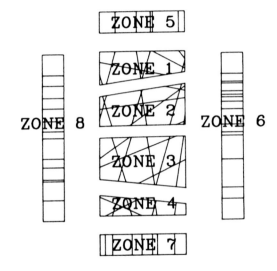

3. Set aside 1½ yards of navy blue for backing.

   All pattern pieces are marked with a circle indicating which color material is to be used. The solid circle represents navy blue; the dotted one, turquoise; the cross-hatched, green; and the empty one, lavender. Pin patterns to fabric and cut carefuly. Cut one element from every pattern piece unless noted otherwise.

   Cut a long edge strip, 2″ wide and 14′ long, from navy blue material.

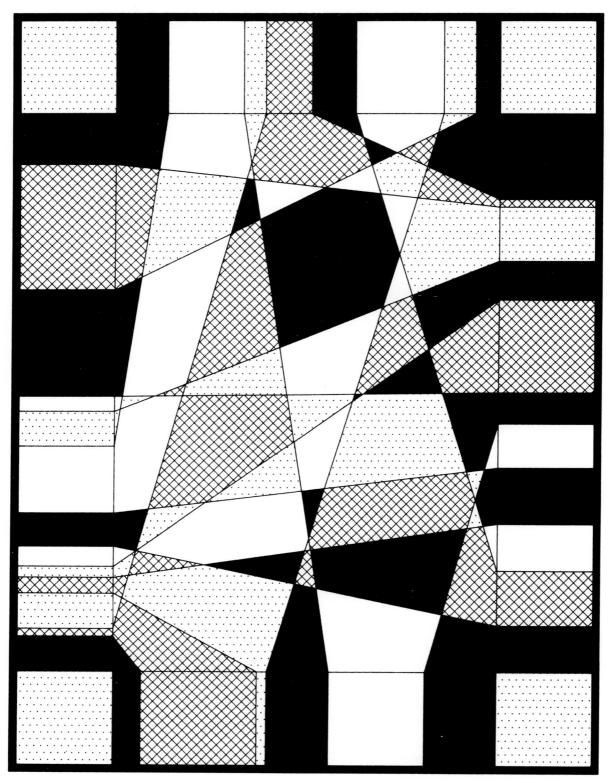

Finished quilt, 36" by 48"

4. Each pattern piece has the numbers of adjoining pieces written along the edges.

   Sew the elements of each zone together. Zone 1 has elements 1 to 13 in it. Zone 2 has elements 14 to 37. Zone 3 has elements 38 to 55. Zone 4 has elements 56 to 69.

   Sew the four zones together, matching seams carefully.

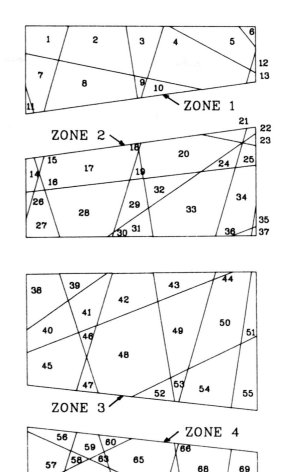

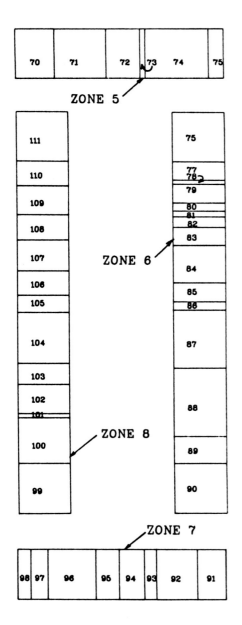

5. Sew the border zones together. Zone 5 has elements 70 to 75. Zone 6 begins and ends with corner squares 76 and 90, with elements 77 to 89 between. Zone 7 has elements 91 to 98. Zone 8 begins and ends with corner squares 99 and 111, with elements 100 to 110 between.

   Sew the border zones to the quilt zones already assembled, matching seams carefully. Sew zones 5 and 7 first, then finish with zones 6 and 8.

6. Lay the quilt backing, face down, on a large table or work surface. Lay the batting on top of it. Lay the quilt top, right side up, on top of the batting. Pin through all three layers, smoothing them to eliminate wrinkles or bumps. Machine stitch along the edge of the quilt top. Trim close to the seam.

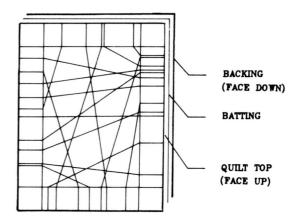

BACKING
(FACE DOWN)

BATTING

QUILT TOP
(FACE UP)

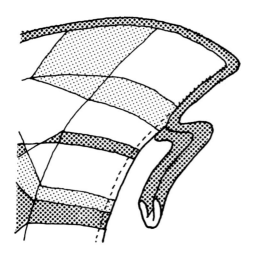

7. Press the seam allowances of the edge strip under. Hand stitch the strip around the quilt assembly.

8. For quilting the three layers together, sew around each quilt element just inside its seam lines. Use thread that matches the element.

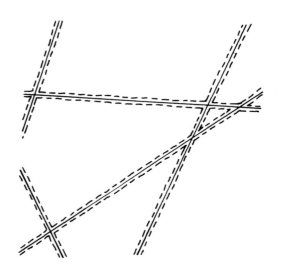

Pattern Pieces

Shown one-half actual size

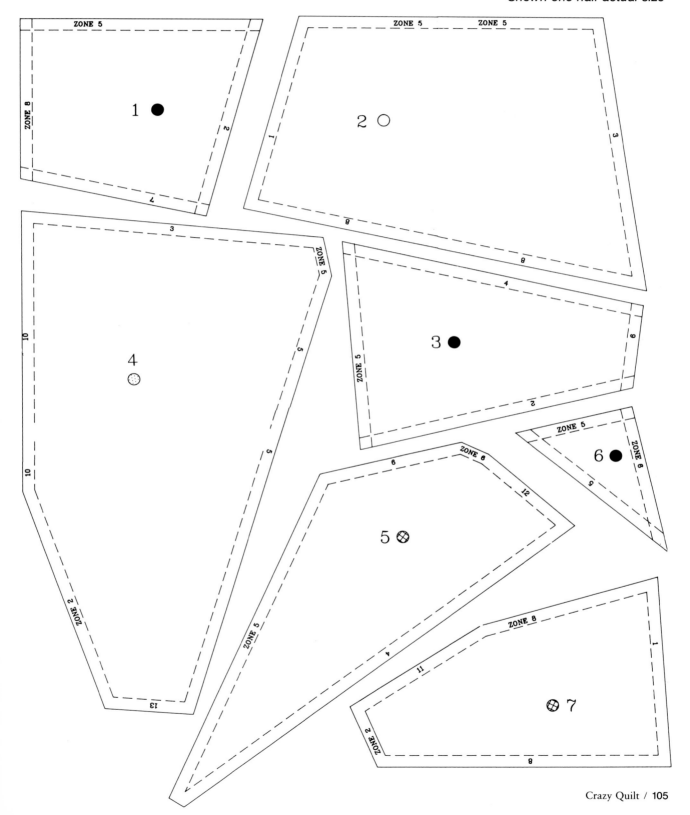

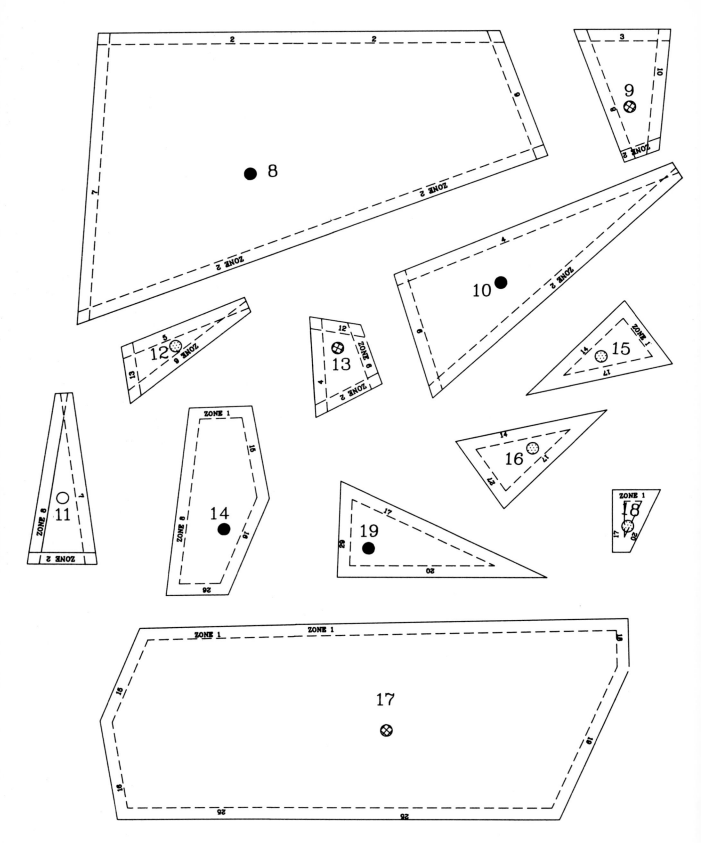

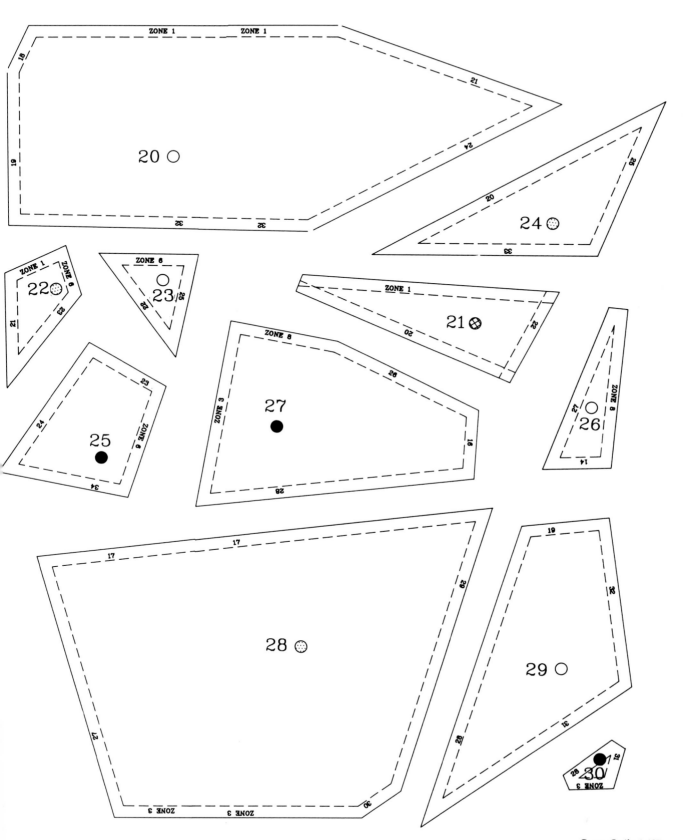

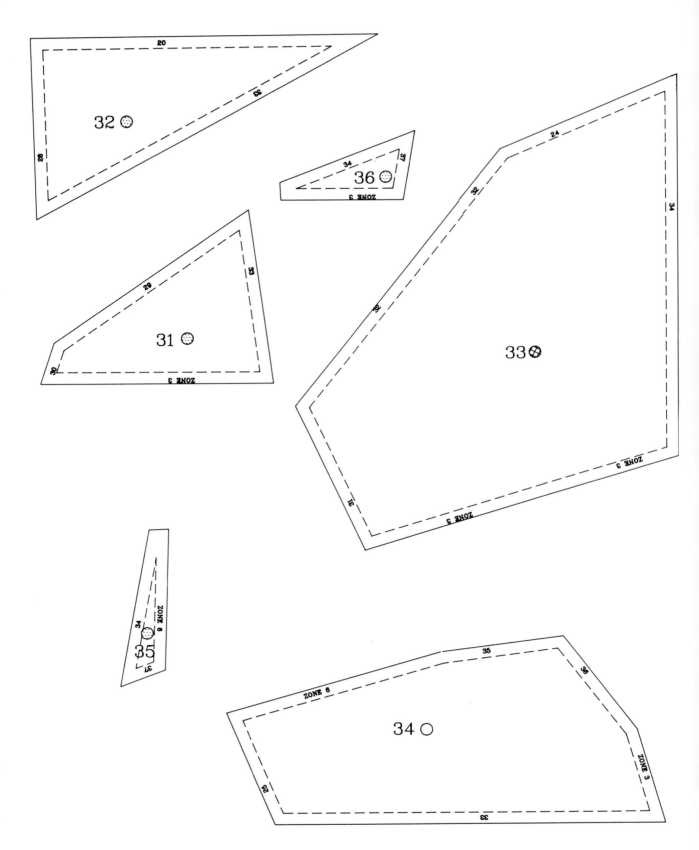

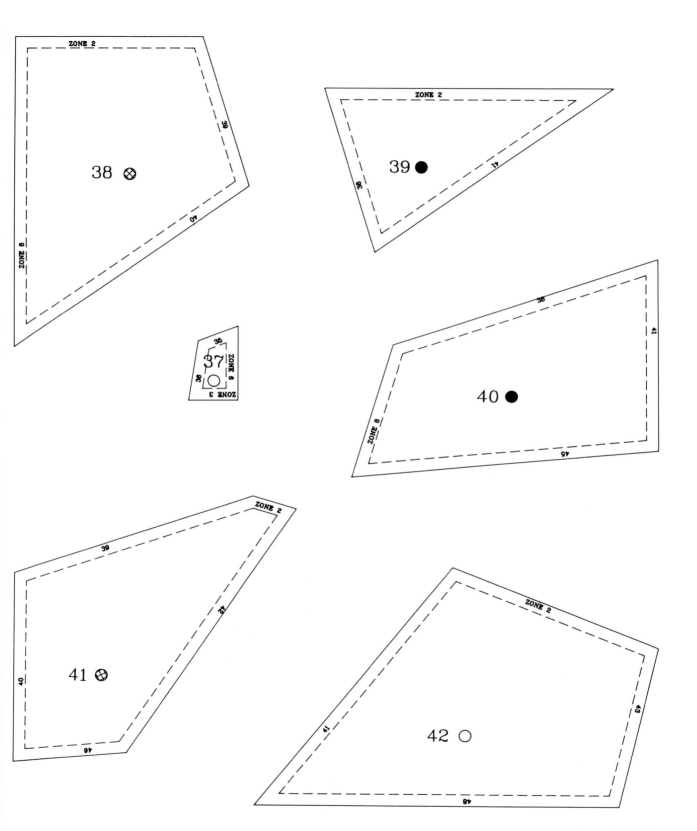

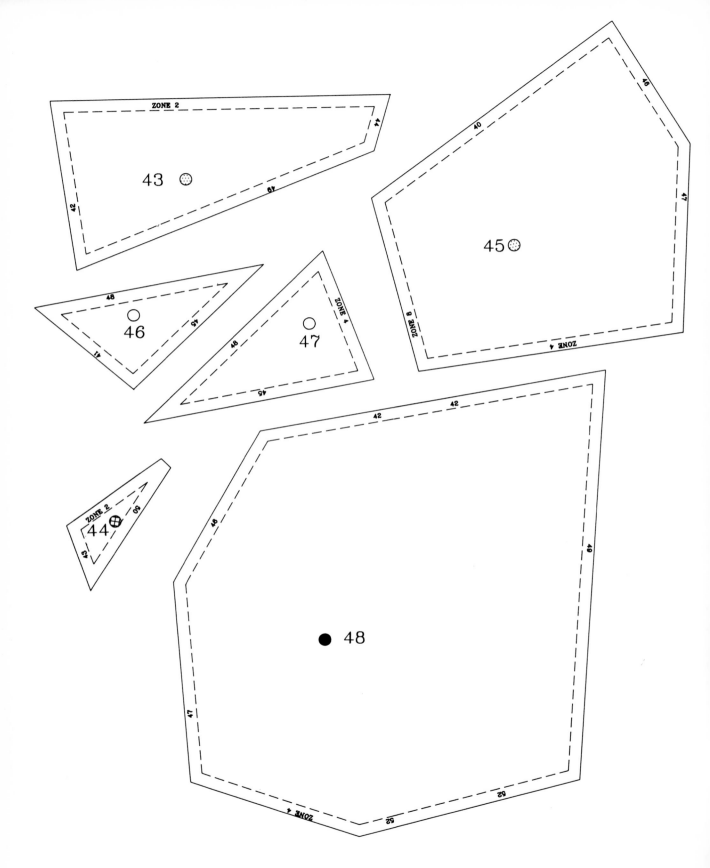

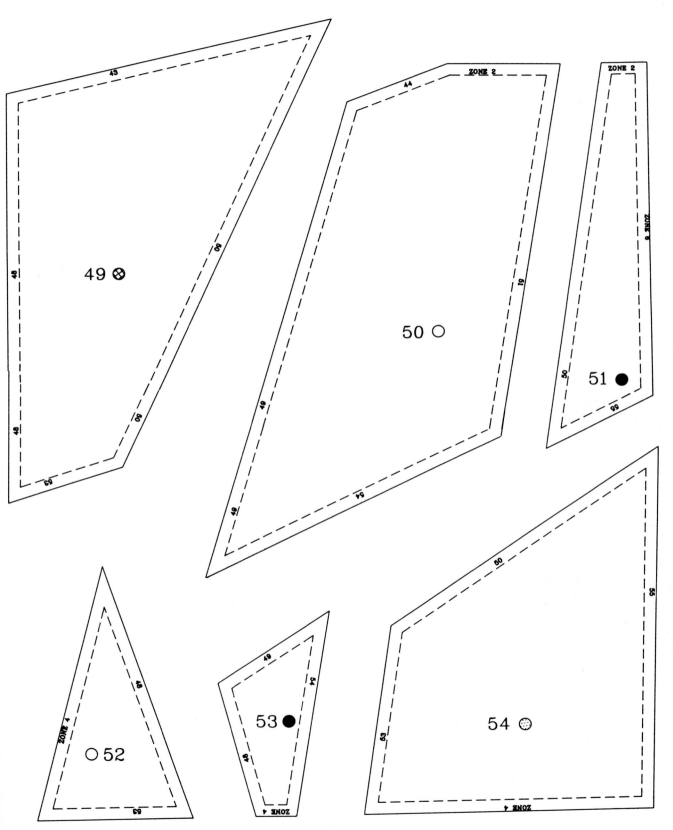

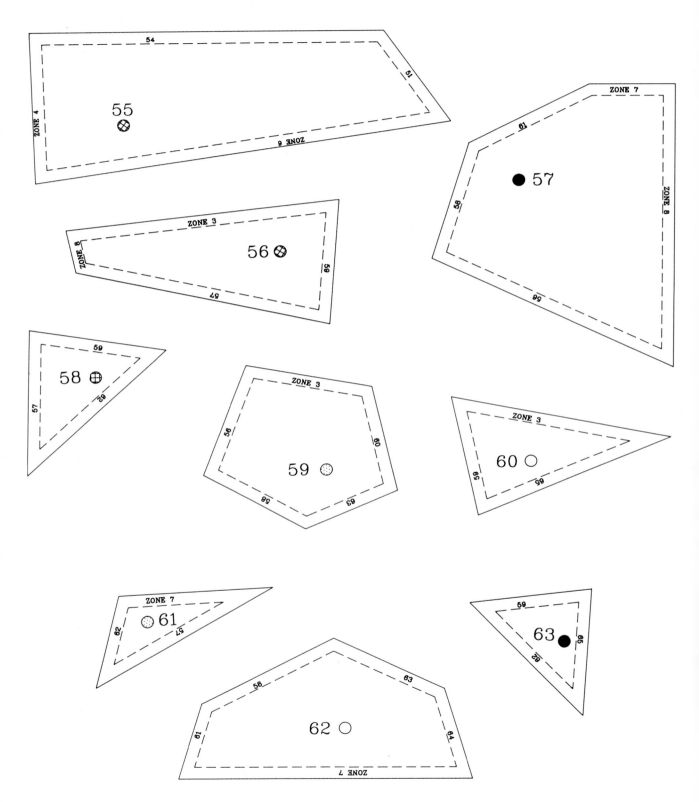

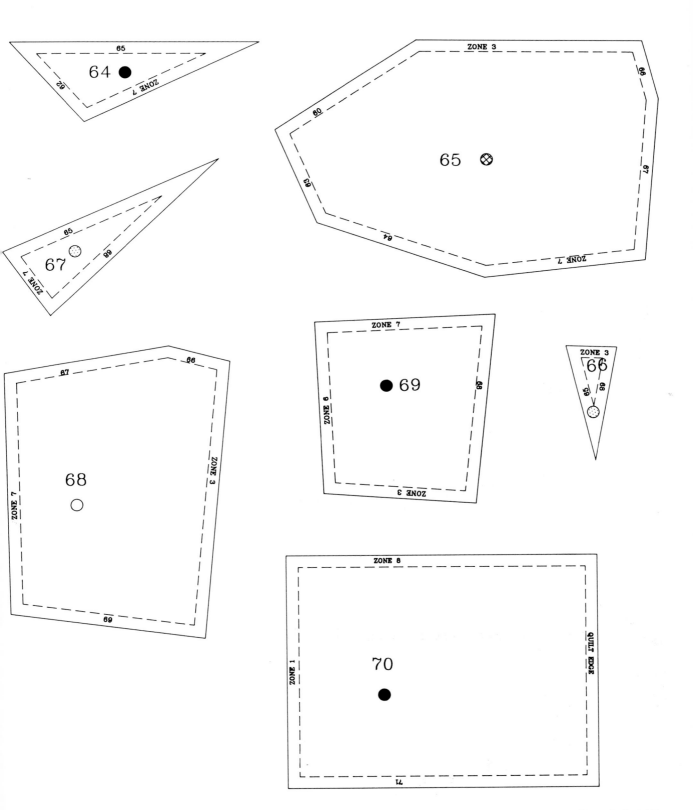

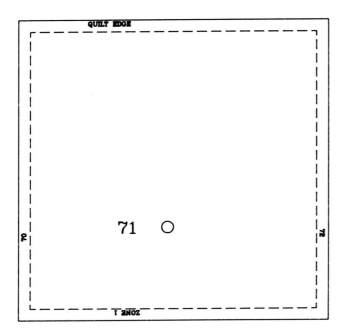

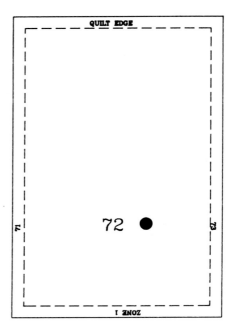

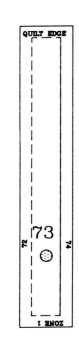

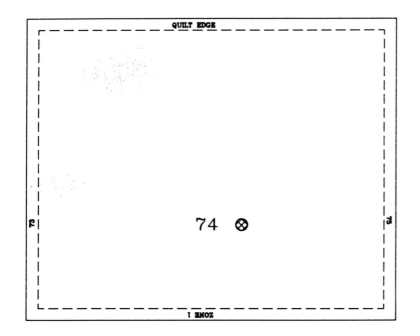

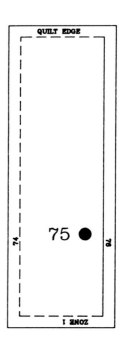

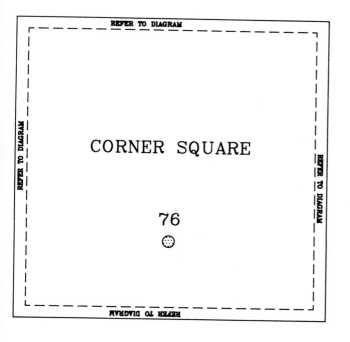

REFER TO DIAGRAM

CORNER SQUARE

76

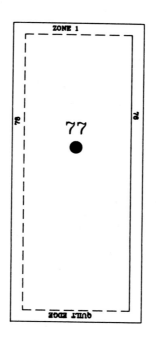

ZONE 1

77

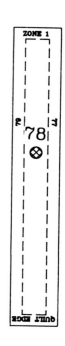

ZONE 1

78

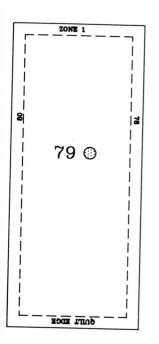

ZONE 1

79

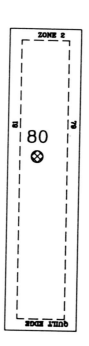

ZONE 2

80

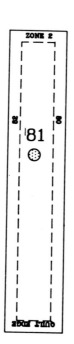

ZONE 2

81

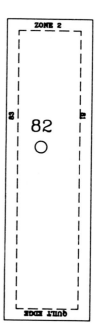

ZONE 2

82

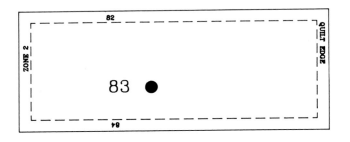

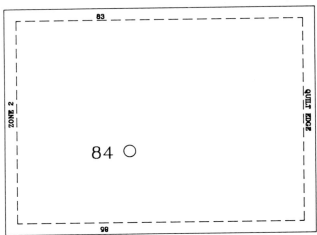

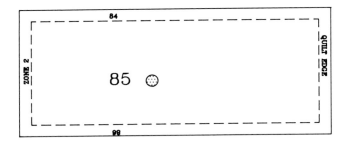

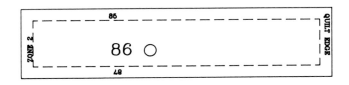

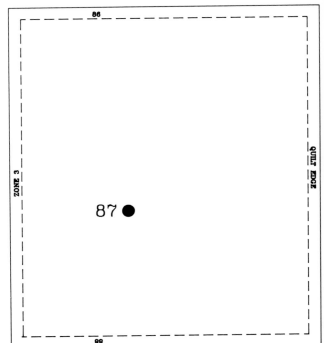

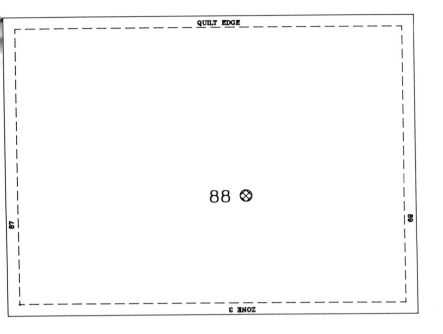

88 ⊗

QUILT EDGE

87

89

ZONE 3

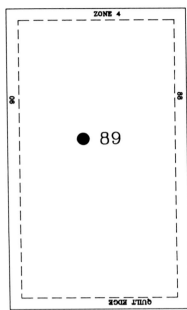

ZONE 4

90

88

89 ●

QUILT EDGE

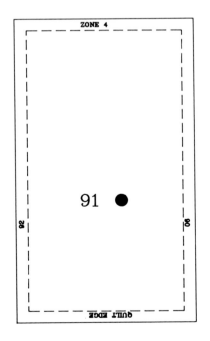

ZONE 4

92

90

91 ●

QUILT EDGE

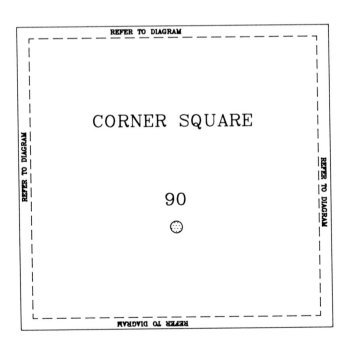

REFER TO DIAGRAM

CORNER SQUARE

90

REFER TO DIAGRAM

REFER TO DIAGRAM

REFER TO DIAGRAM

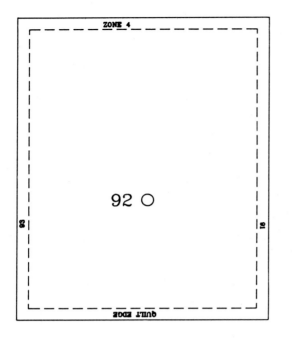

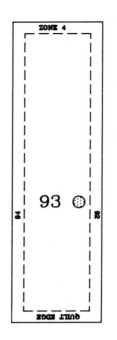

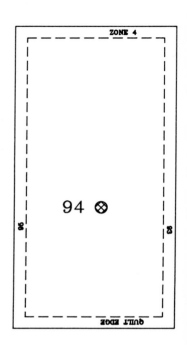

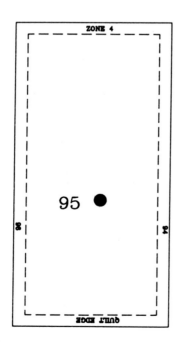

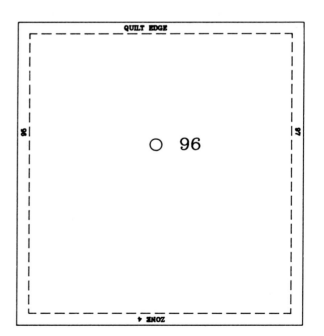

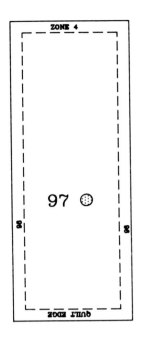

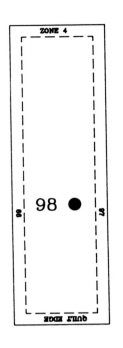

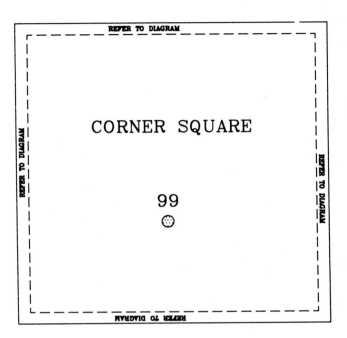

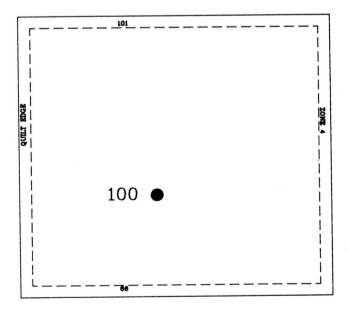

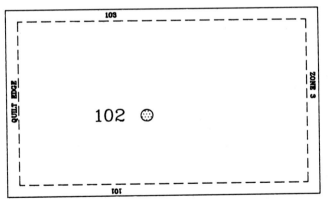

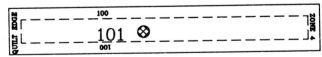

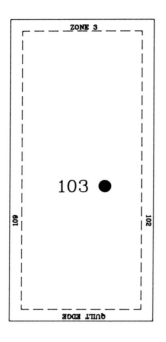

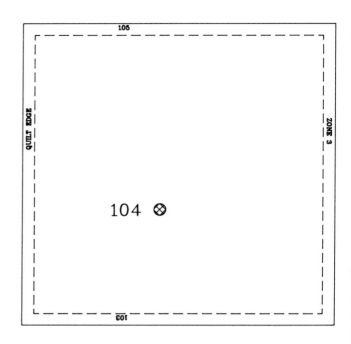

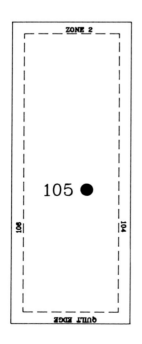

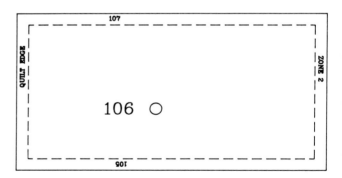

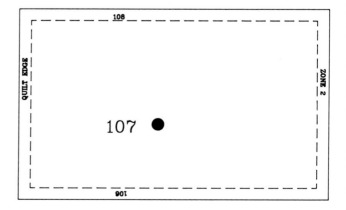

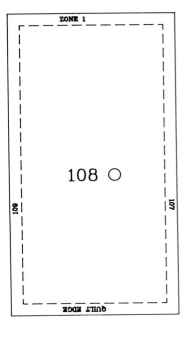

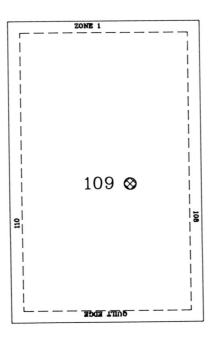

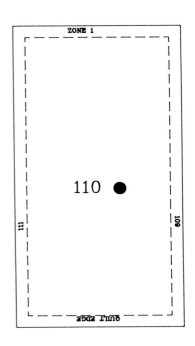

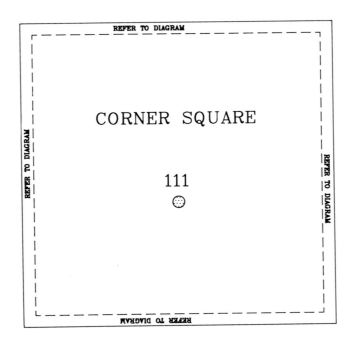

Finished quilt, 38" by 52"

10. Watermelons

The watermelon is summer's most distinctive fruit. It suggests picnics, holidays, and family gatherings. It has remarkable visual appeal. It cuts cleanly into a circle, semicircle, or wedge. Each piece has neatly arranged dark seeds set into the redness of the melon and protected by a mottled green rind.

With these qualities and associations it is not surprising that watermelons show up in folk art, paintings, and carvings. But they appear only rarely in quilts, and then either as an embroidered image lost on the surface of a crazy quilt, or deformed into a triangular piecework shape to fit into the overall pattern.

This simple design sets a quarter circle of plain red cloth—calicoes or prints would diminish the effect—against a printed green background. Recessed beyond the face of the melon are the seeds, made of dark printed material and done in reverse appliqué. Two nested arcs, one white and one plain green, complete the unit. It is important that the fabrics on the cut face of the melon are plain and those beyond it are prints. This differentiates between the two surfaces, pushes the printed elements back from the visual surface, and makes the design sharper and crisper.

Like most asymmetric units in other quilt designs, the melon blocks could be combined in several different ways. The blocks could be assembled to make full-circle melons or half-circle melons. The version illustrated here is less representational. All the squares have the same orientation, and the quarter-circle melons make an arrangement reminiscent of fan quilts of the Victorian period.

Instructions

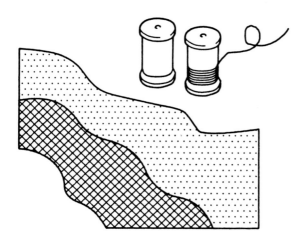

1. Materials:

   1 yard of solid red (watermelon centers)
   1 yard black print (seeds)
   ½ yard each of solid white and light
       green (inner and outer rinds)
   3 yards green print (skin and backing)
   Cotton batting
   White and green thread
   5 yards of black piping

2. Pin patterns to fabric. Cut carefully.

   From the green print, cut two border strips, 2″ wide and 36″ long. Cut two more, 2″ wide and 50″ long.

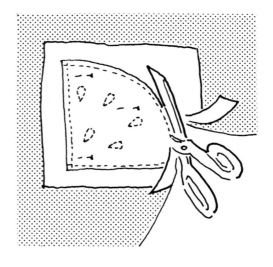

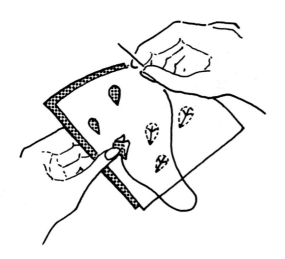

3. The watermelon seeds are reverse appliqué. Pin the red cloth over the black print. Cut a hole for each seed as shown on the pattern. Stitch along the seam line.

4. Sew the white and green arcs to the red and black quarter-circles.

   Sew the green print skin to the light green outer rind. Clip seams as required.

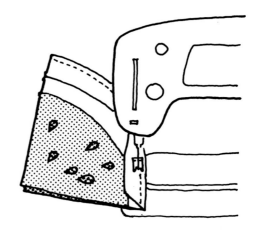

5. Sew the watermelon blocks into rows. Sew the rows together, matching all seams carefully.

6. Pin the piping to the edges of the watermelon assembly. Sew the border strips and piping to the quilt top.

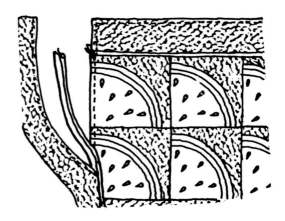

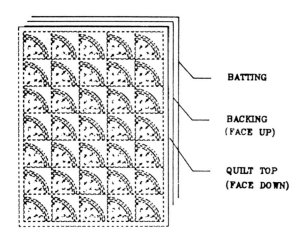

BATTING

BACKING
(FACE UP)

QUILT TOP
(FACE DOWN)

7. Lay the quilt batting on a large table or work area. Lay the backing, face up, on top of the batting. Lay the quilt top, face down, on the backing. Pin through all three layers. Machine stitch along the edge of the quilt top, leaving an 8″ gap at the end. Trim close to the seam.

8. Turn the quilt by pulling it through the 8″ gap. Sew the gap closed by hand.

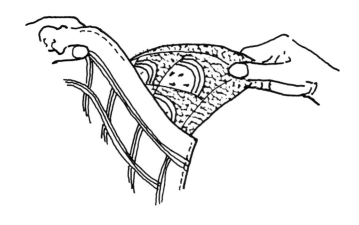

9. For quilting the three layers together, hand stitch a quarter circle that follows the edges of the red watermelon center to the light green outer rind. Then stitch along the edges of the skin element. Finally, sew diagonal lines, 1″ apart, through the green skin as shown.

Pattern Pieces

Shown one-half actual size

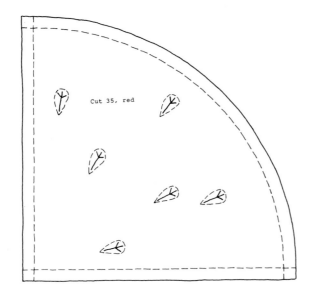

Cut 35, red

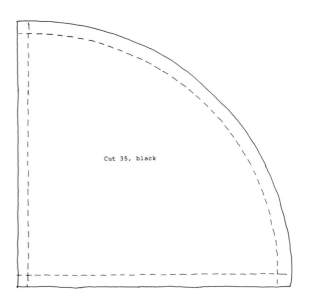

Cut 35, black

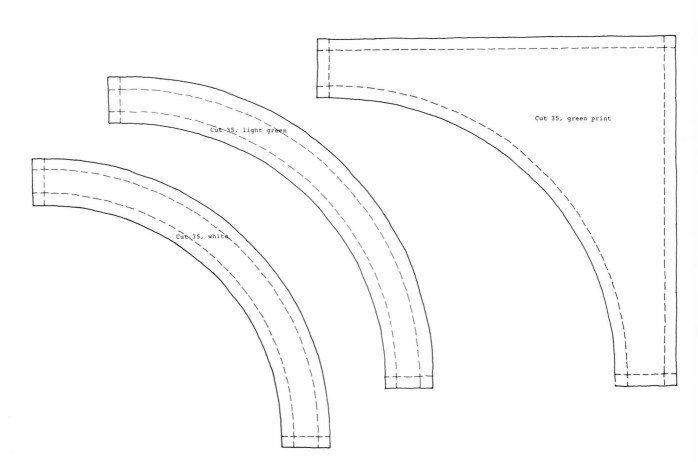

Cut 35, light green

Cut 35, white

Cut 35, green print

11. Fence Rail

Certain quilt patterns generate optical illusions. They create the appearance of motion or turbulence, or the suggestion of three dimensions. Typically, these illusions depend on pattern asymmetries, either in color, tone, or line. In spite of the complexity of the illusion, the lines of these quilts are usually very simple.

Among the most striking examples are the Tumbling Blocks design, the Pinwheel quilts, and the Log Cabin and Fence Rail groups. In the Tumbling Blocks pattern, identical diamond-shaped pieces are colored with light, dark, and intermediate tones. The blocks appear to tumble off the surface of the quilt because of the arrangement of shades. If the elements were colored uniformly, or even randomly, the dynamic would be lost. Pinwheel quilts, including designs like Crazy Ann and Whirlwind, rely on anti-symmetry to suggest turbulence and motion. They are usually composed of triangular elements and executed in two colors. As with the Tumbling Blocks design, the arrangement of colors is critical. Were the triangular pieces done in different tones, the illusion would be gone. The Log Cabin and Fence Rail patterns are inherently symmetrical, and depend for effect on coloring. The actual lines of these designs are simple— both are composed entirely of strip elements.

Fence Rail has only one block. It is a square divided into three bands. The blocks are sewn together in such a way that vertical and horizontal bands alternate. The visual power of the quilt comes when the bands of similar color or tone join up across the block seams to create zigzag lines.

This version of Fence Rail acknowledges, even encourages, this reading by using a strong orange-red shade for the dominant zigzag color. A secondary line is cream. The third color—it is the middle stripe in each block unit—is dark gray. The dark gray bands do not join up because of the red and cream elements. They do not form a jagged line, only an interrupted one. On this surface, the solid dark color seems to be a deep shadow of the other lines.

Finished quilt, 37" by 46"

Instructions

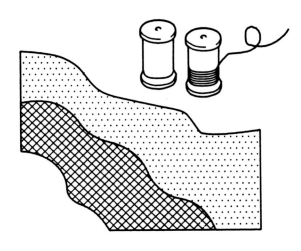

1. Materials:
   2¼ yards solid red cloth
   ¾ yard solid gray cloth
   ¾ yard solid cream cloth
   Cotton batting
   Cream and red thread

2. Set aside 1½ yards of red cloth for quilt backing.

   Cut the remaining red cloth into 9 strips, 2″ wide, 45″ long.

   Cut the cream cloth into 9 strips, 2″ wide, 45 ″ long.

   Cut the gray cloth into 9 strips, 2″ wide, 45 ″ long.

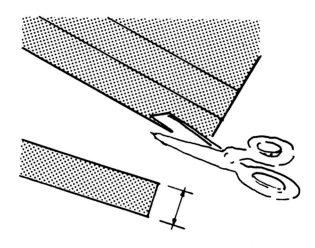

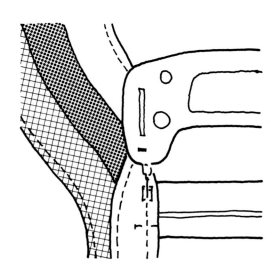

3. Sew the strips together in groups of three. Each group should begin with a red strip, then have the gray one, and then the cream one.

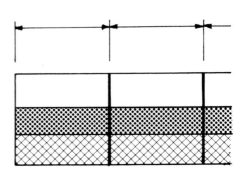

4. Measure and cut across the seams in the strips just sewn. Cut 9 squares from each strip. The squares will be 5″ by 5″.

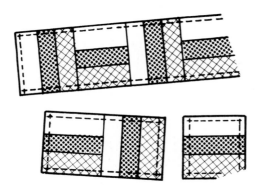

5. Sew 8 squares together to make a strip of squares. Alternate the squares as shown. There will be ten strips of squares, five of which begin with vertical elements and five with horizontal ones. There will be one extra square left over; discard it.

Assemble the quilt top by sewing the strips of squares together, matching seams carefully.

6. On a large table or work surface, lay the quilt batting down. Lay the backing material, face up, on top of the batting. Lay the quilt top, face down, on the backing. Pin around the edges.

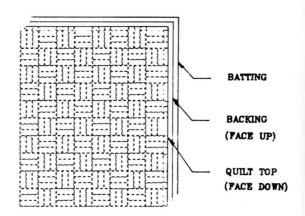

BATTING

BACKING
(FACE UP)

QUILT TOP
(FACE DOWN)

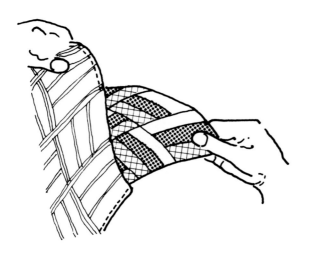

7. Sew around the edges, leaving an 8″ gap at the end. Trim the seams.

   Use the 8″ gap to turn the quilt right side out.

   Hand sew the 8″ gap closed.

8. To emphasize the geometry of the quilt, hand stitch along the edges of the red and cream elements as shown.

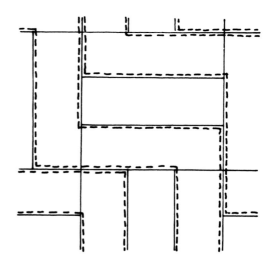

12. Apple Pie

Geometric quilt patterns are those which use regular geometric elements—squares, rectangles, and triangles—in some consistent overall organization. In the long history of geometric designs the individual variations are too numerous to count. But certain families of patterns can be identified. For example, the Log Cabin family uses long strips to make various types of blocks. Courthouse Steps, Windmill Blades, and Pineapples are members of this group.

The Apple Pie quilt belongs to a family in which each block has a central rotated square. This pattern has some similarities to the "Shoo-fly Pie" pattern of Amish quilters. Central rotated squares are flanked by triangles and strips. The corners of the strips are broken down into little triangles. These tiny triangles are the "flies" which buzz around each pie.

Early quilts were often done in contrasting prints, most often in a dark blue and a white calico print. Printed cloth was a manufactured good, not always easy to get, and certainly not available in the rainbow of shades and patterns offered in stores today. A bolt or two, bought once a year, would be used for that year's dresses, shirts, quilts, and curtains.

A limit of two colors was not a hardship for pioneer quilters. Their quilts are as rich and interesting as some of the later ones that exploit a wider palette.

The quilt stitching for this piece superimposes four concentric circles over the blue-and-white squares. The circles are one inch apart. The first circle fits just inside the central rotated square, and the successive ones cross through the strip and triangular elements.

Instructions

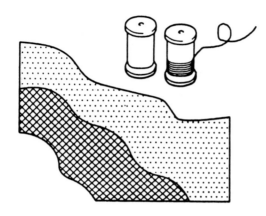

1. Materials:

   2¼ yards dark blue print
   1½ yards white and blue print
   Cotton batting
   Blue yarn or thread for tacking

2. Set aside 1½ yards of dark blue print cloth for quilt backing.

   Pin pattern pieces to cloth. Cut carefully.

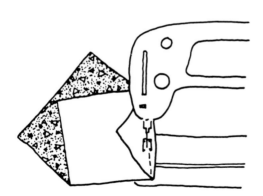

3. Sew the large triangles to the large squares to make the rotated square units. Sew the twelve thin strips and twelve small triangles around the rotated squares to make the blocks.

4. Sew the blocks and lattice strips together to make rows of squares. Sew the lattice strips and squares together to make lattice strips.

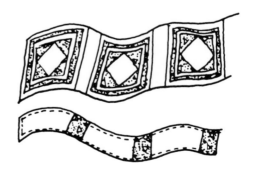

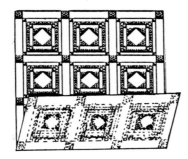

5. Assemble quilt top from rows of squares and lattice strips, matching seams carefully.

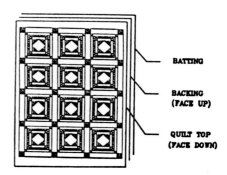

6. On a large table or work surface, lay the quilt batting down. Lay the backing material, face up, on top of the batting. Lay the quilt top, face down, on the backing. Pin around the edges.

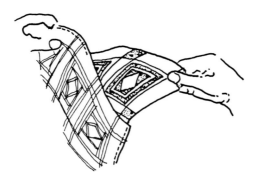

7. Sew around the edges, leaving an 8″ gap at the end. Trim the seams.

   Use the 8″ gap to turn the quilt right side out.

   Hand sew the 8″ gap closed.

8. For quilting, stitch four concentric circles one inch apart on the blue-and-white squares. The first circle begins inside the central rotated square, and the successive ones cross through the strips.

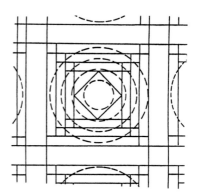

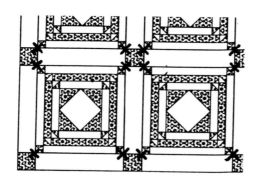

9. Using the heavy blue thread, tack quilt layers together at the corners of the pie blocks.

Finished quilt, 34" by 45"

Pattern Pieces

Shown one-half actual size

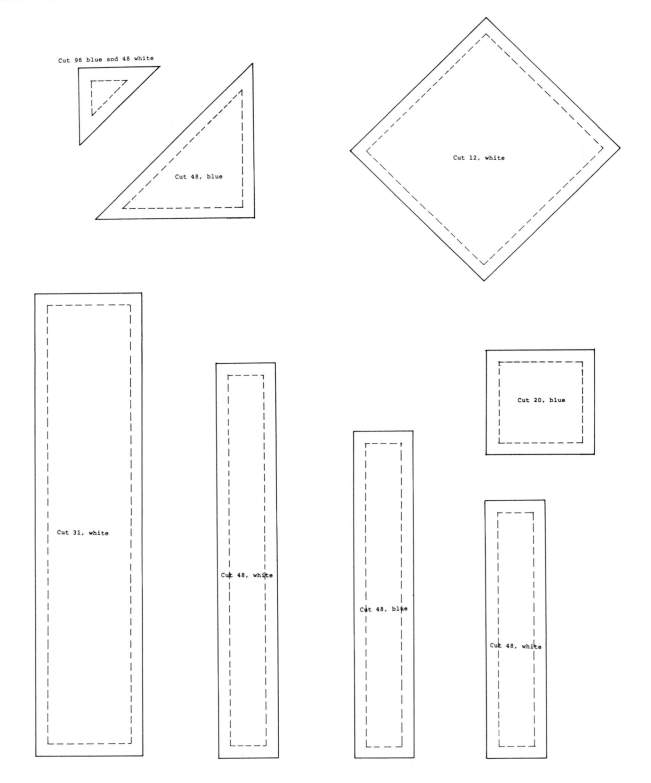

Cut 96 blue and 48 white

Cut 48, blue

Cut 12, white

Cut 31, white

Cut 48, white

Cut 48, blue

Cut 20, blue

Cut 48, white

13. Fire

Three-dimensional quilts are rare. The techniques of using stitching and stuffing to create high and low points are very demanding and difficult. There are two basic methods for creating three-dimensional relief. The first method, known as trapunto, uses top and bottom cloth layers that lie flat against each other. The stitching and varying amounts of stuffing create the three-dimensional effect. The second method is a sculptural one. In sculptural quilts, the top cloth does not lay flatly against the bottom one. It has built-in, sewn-in valleys and ridges. The stuffing fills the volume between the top and bottom cloths, and the stitching holds the quilt together.

The fire quilt is a three-dimensional, sculptural piece. It uses four solid materials—red, orange, gold, and yellow—to make a field of low-relief pyramids. Each pyramid is independently stuffed.

The quilted surface is lively and active. The colors and shapes dazzle the eye. The texture and contour become especially apparent when the quilt is draped or folded.

Solid colors enhance the three-dimensional effect. Prints would tend to obscure the lines. They would superimpose a fine pattern which would read across the edge and vertices, and which would effectively flatten the surface. In this quilt, the colors also intensify the low relief by implying shade and highlight.

This design could be executed in many different colors. In blue and purple shades it might resemble jewels; in whites the effect would be like ice and snow. Here, the reds, yellows, and oranges are used to suggest the colors of hot coals and embers. The whole quilt has the glow and tone of fire.

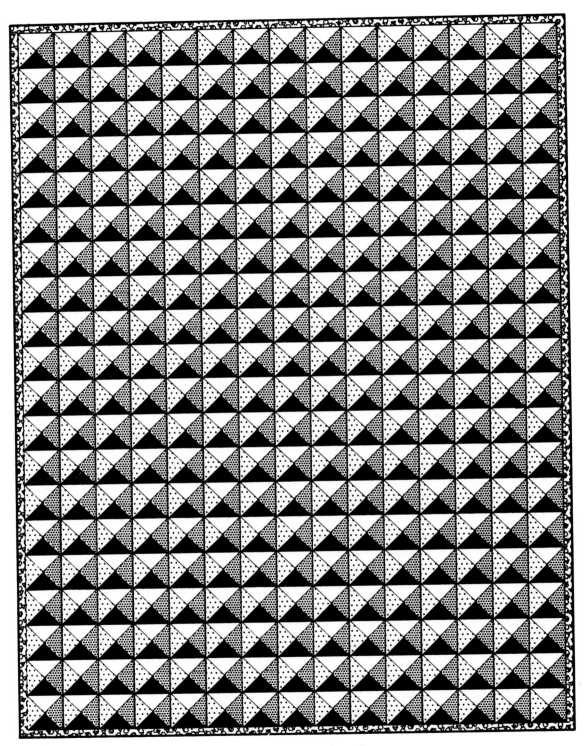

Finished quilt, 35" by 47"

Instructions

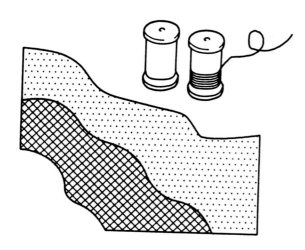

1. Materials:

   ¾ yard each of solid yellow, gold, orange, and red

   1¾ yards of red and orange print

   Cotton batting in both quilt and stuffing form

   Orange and red thread

2. Cut triangular pieces from solid colored fabrics. The easiest way to do this is to cut 2¼″-wide strips and then to cut a series of triangles from each strip.

   Cut a long edge strip, 4″ wide and 14′ long, from the printed material.

3. Sew the triangles together to make pyramids. Note that the pyramids will not lie flat.

   All the pyramids should have the same arrangement of colors—going clockwise from the top, yellow, gold, red, orange.

4. Sew the pyramids together into strips with the red elements at the bottom. There are 15 pyramids in each strip.

   Sew the strips together, matching seams carefully.

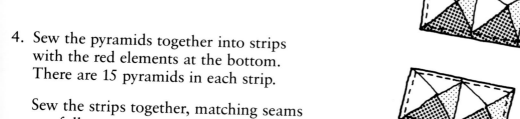

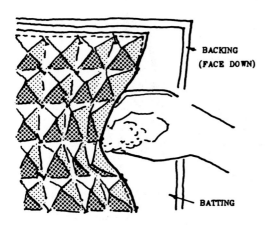

BACKING
(FACE DOWN)

BATTING

5. Lay the quilt backing face down, on a large table or work area. Lay the batting on top of it. Lay the quilt top on it, right side up, and pin through all three layers along the orange edge of the top. Insert a clump of stuffing between the quilt top and the batting under the first pyramid and pin at all corners. Repeat until all pyramids are stuffed.

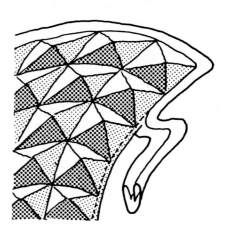

6. Using the red and orange thread, sew by hand along all the valleys between the pyramids. Trim the quilt assembly around its edges.

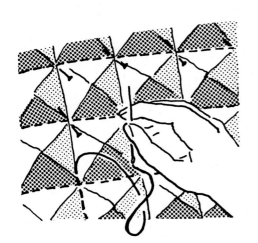

7. Press the seam allowances of the edge strip under. Hand stitch the strip around the quilt assembly.

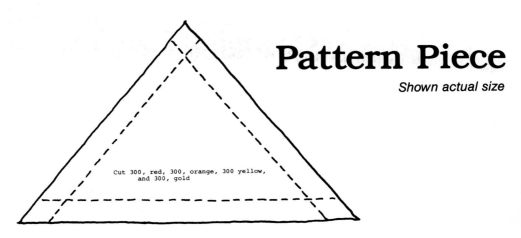

Pattern Piece

Shown actual size

Cut 300, red, 300, orange, 300 yellow, and 300, gold

Finished quilt, 40″ by 50″

14. Waves

Very few pieced quilts have curving lines. The curve is both difficult to work with and uneconomical to cut. Orange Peel, Steeplechase, and Drunkard's Path are among the few traditional pieced, curved designs.

This quilt uses two solid colors and a simple, shallow arc in each block. The arc joins with adjacent inverted arcs to create regular wave patterns.

The design would be rather flat without the quilting. Stitching lines one inch apart run across the waves, mirroring the crests and troughs. The stitching is done in alternating bands of blue and white to match the fabrics, but the lines appear and disappear as they cross from white to blue at the wave lines. The stitching bands are five lines wide; that is, there are five white lines followed by five blue.

Instructions

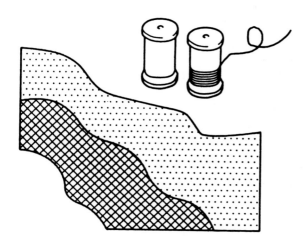

1. Materials:

   2½ yards of solid blue cloth
   1 yard of white cloth
   Cotton batting
   White and blue thread

2. Set aside 1½ yards of blue cloth for backing.

   Pin patterns to fabric. Cut carefully.

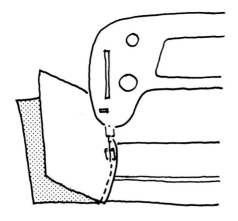

3. Sew white and blue pieces together to make blocks. Clip along curves as required.

4. Sew blocks together to make rows, matching seams at the waves.

   Assemble blocks to make quilt top, matching seams carefully.

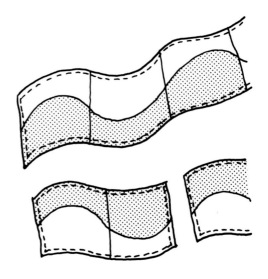

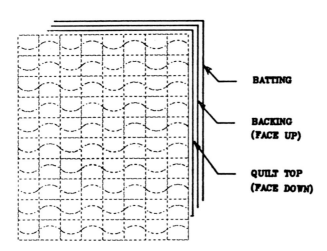

BATTING

BACKING
(FACE UP)

QUILT TOP
(FACE DOWN)

5. Lay the quilt batting on a large table or work area. Lay the backing, face up, on top of the batting. Lay the quilt top, face down, on the backing. Pin through all three layers. Machine stitch along the edge of the quilt top, leaving an 8″ gap at the end. Trim close to the seam.

6. Turn the quilt by pulling it through the 8″ gap. Sew the gap closed by hand.

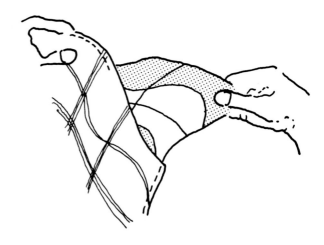

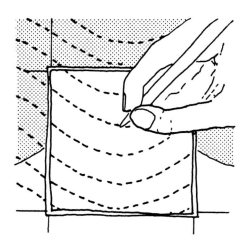

7. Mark quilting lines on the quilt top, using stitching pattern and quilter's marking paper. The quilting stitching runs across the wave lines as shown.

8. Stitch along the quilting lines. Use white thread for the first five quilting lines, then use blue thread for the next five lines. Alternate thread colors until entire quilt is quilted.

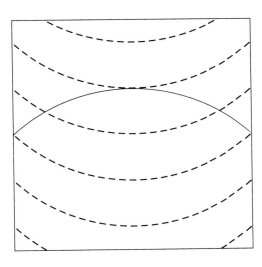

Pattern Pieces

Shown actual size

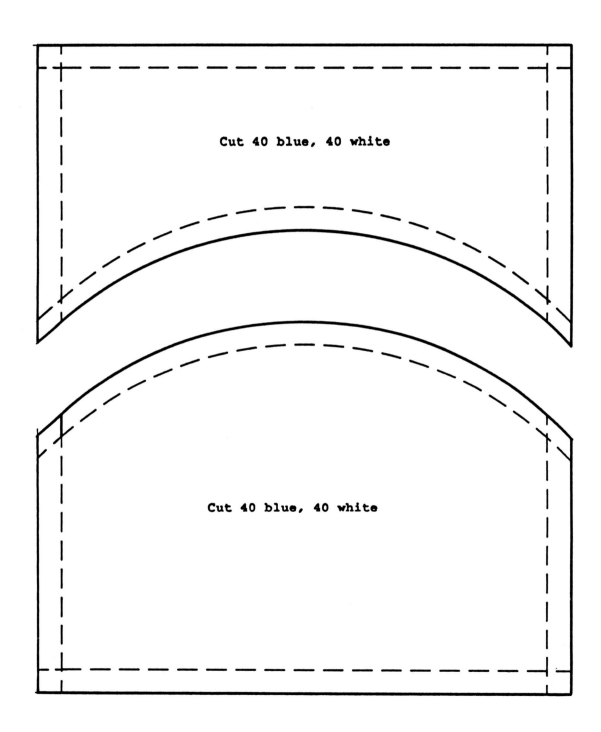

Cut 40 blue, 40 white

Cut 40 blue, 40 white

15. Pinwheels

The Pinwheels pattern is a member of a large family of spiraling, illusionistic designs. Other members of the group include Old Maid's Puzzle, Windmill, Seesaw, and Next-Door Neighbor. All these designs lack familiar axial symmetry: each block has a rotational symmetry instead.

This quilt is intense and dark—the red pinwheels jar against the blue/black field. As in Amish quilts, the darkness of the field sparks the quilt surface and makes the red seem extra vivid. This quilt departs from Amish traditions in its use of printed fabrics rather than solid colors. The prints are subtle ones. Fine black lines, in an irregular crackled network, add texture to the red and blue forms.

The whole quilt has a jagged, unsettled quality to it, rather like graffiti.

Finished quilt, 34" by 45"

Instructions

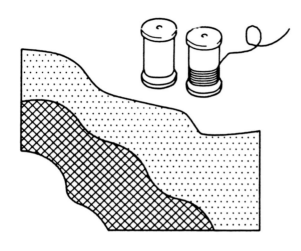

1. Materials:

    3½ yards dark blue print
    2½ yards bright red print
    Cotton batting
    Blue yarn or thread for tacking

2. Set aside 1½ yards of dark blue print cloth for quilt backing. Pin pattern pieces to cloth. Cut carefully.

    Cut 2 blue border strips, 2½″ wide and 41½″ long, and 2 additional blue border strips, 2½″ wide and 34½″ long.

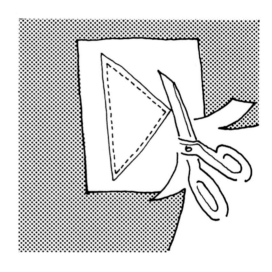

3. Sew the triangles and quadrilaterals together to make pinwheel blocks as shown.

4. Sew the pinwheels together to make a strip of blocks. Assemble the strips of pinwheels to make the quilt top.

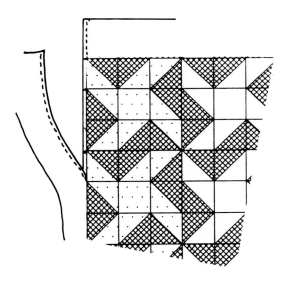

5. Sew border strips to edges of the quilt top.

6. On a large table or work surface, lay the quilt batting down. Lay the backing material, face up, on top of the batting. Lay the quilt top, face down, on the backing. Pin around the edges.

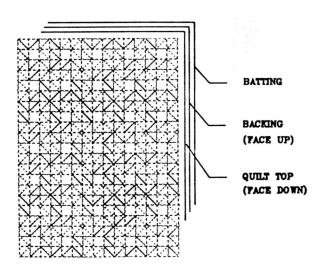

BATTING

BACKING
(FACE UP)

QUILT TOP
(FACE DOWN)

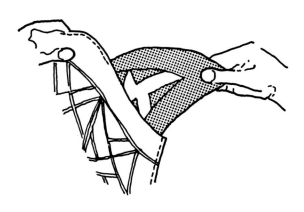

7. Sew around the edges, leaving an 8″ gap at the end. Trim the seams. Use the 8″ gap to turn the quilt right side out. Hand sew the 8″ gap closed.

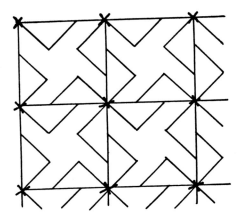

8. Using the heavy blue thread, tack quilt layers together at the corners of each pinwheel block.

Pattern Pieces

Shown actual size

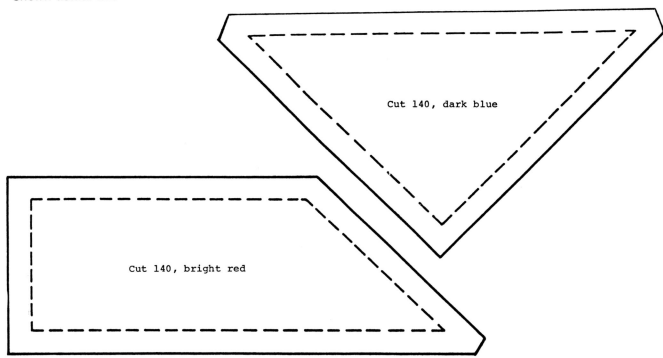

Cut 140, dark blue

Cut 140, bright red

Acknowledgments

The following people and institutions were particularly helpful to me while I did research on the history and design of crib quilts: Anita Jones and Nancy Press of the Baltimore Museum of Art, Leona Bicker of the Brooklyn Museum, Janey Fine of the Museum of American Folk Art, Barb Abrams of the Germantown Historical Society, Amelia Peck of the Metropolitan Museum of Art, Blanche Greenstein of Thomas K. Woodard Antiques, Laura Fisher of Laura Fisher Antiques, and Faith Ringgold and Jan Myers, both of them quilt makers.

At The Main Street Press, Lawrence Grow, Vicki Brooks, and Beth Kalet worked to make the manuscript into a book. Photographers William Taylor and Joan Ford took most of the photographs that accompany the quilt projects. The design arrangements in each case were my own work. William Taylor took the pictures for projects 1 and 3 through 14. Joan Ford photographed quilt project 15. Three young models posed with certain quilts. Alexandra Suarez sat with the Hearts and Hands quilt. Megan Ronning posed with the Nine-Patch quilt. And Halley McDaniel posed with the Fence Rail quilt. Sharon McGinness and Steve McDaniel helped with the drawings and sketches.

Bibliography

Bacon, Lenice Ingram. *American Patchwork Quilts*. New York: William Morow, 1973.

Bishop, Robert, and Elizabeth Safanda. *A Gallery of Amish Quilts: Design Diversity from a Plain People*. New York: E. P. Dutton, 1976.

Colby, Averil. *Patchwork Quilts*. New York: Charles Scribner's Sons, 1971.

Cooper, Patricia, and Norma Bradley Buferd. *The Quilters: Women and Domestic Art*. Garden City, N.Y.: Doubleday & Co., 1977.

Fisher, Laura. *Quilts of Illusion*. Pittstown, N.J.: The Main Street Press, 1988.

Gutcheon, Beth. *The Perfect Patchwork Primer*. Baltimore: Penguin Books, Inc. 1974.

Haders, Phyllis. *Sunshine and Shadow: The Amish and their Quilts*. Pittstown, N.J.: The Main Street Press, 1976.

Holstein, Jonathan. *Abstract Design in American Quilts*. New York: The Whitney Museum of American Art, 1971.

————. *The Pieced Quilt: An American Design Tradition*. Greenwich, Conn.: New York Graphic Society, 1973.

————, editor. *Kentucky Quilts 1800-1900*. Louisville: The Kentucky Quilt Project, 1982.

Johnson, Bruce, et al. *A Child's Comfort: Baby and Doll Quilts in American Folk Art,* New York: Harcourt Brace Jovanovich in association with the Museum of American Folk Art, 1977.

McMorris, Penny. *Crazy Quilts*. New York: E. P. Dutton, 1984.

The Quilt Digest. San Francisco: The Quilt Digest Press, 1985.

Pellman, Rachel and Kenneth. *Amish Crib Quilts*. Intercourse, Penna.: Good Books, 1985.

————. *The World of Amish Quilts*. Intercourse, Penna.: Good Books, 1984.

Safford, Carleton, and Robert Bishop. *America's Quilts and Coverlets*. New York: E. P. Dutton, 1972.

Schorsch, Anita. *Images of Childhood*. Pittstown, N.J.: The Main Street Press, 1979.

Woodard, Thomas K. and Blanche Greenstein. *Crib Quilts and Other Small Wonders*. New York: E. P. Dutton, 1981.